REPRINTS OF ECONOMIC CLASSICS

ESSAYS on GOVERNMENT, JURIS-
PRUDENCE, LIBERTY OF THE
PRESS & LAW OF NATIONS

ESSAYS

ON

GOVERNMENT

JURISPRUDENCE

LIBERTY OF THE PRESS

AND

LAW OF NATIONS

BY

JAMES MILL

REPRINTS OF ECONOMIC CLASSICS

AUGUSTUS M. KELLEY · PUBLISHERS

These essays were written for the Supplement of
the Encyclopedia Britannica and appeared in the
years 1816-1823.

First Innes edition, 1825
(London: J. Innes, Printer, 1825)

Reprinted 1986 by
Augustus M. Kelley, Publishers
Fairfield NJ 07006

Library of Congress Cataloging-in-Publication Data

Mill, James, 1773-1836.
    Essays on government, jurisprudence, liberty of
the press, and law of nations.

    Reprint. Originally published: London : J. Innes,
Printer, 1825
    1. Political science. 2. Law--History and criticism.
3. Freedom of the press. I. Title.
JC223.M64   1986   320   86-7454
ISBN 0-678-00297-5

Manufactured in the United States of America

ESSAYS

ON

GOVERNMENT,

JURISPRUDENCE,

LIBERTY OF THE PRESS,

AND

LAW OF NATIONS.

WRITTEN FOR

𝕿𝖍𝖊 𝕾𝖚𝖕𝖕𝖑𝖊𝖒𝖊𝖓𝖙 𝖙𝖔 𝖙𝖍𝖊 𝕰𝖓𝖈𝖞𝖈𝖑𝖔𝖕æ𝖉𝖎𝖆 𝕭𝖗𝖎𝖙𝖆𝖓𝖓𝖎𝖈𝖆,

AND PRINTED BY PERMISSION OF

THE PROPRIETORS OF THE ENCYCLOPÆDIA.

BY JAMES MILL, ESQ.
AUTHOR OF THE HISTORY OF BRITISH INDIA.

NOT FOR SALE.

𝕷𝖔𝖓𝖉𝖔𝖓:

THE ARTICLE

GOVERNMENT,

REPRINTED FROM

THE SUPPLEMENT

TO THE

ENCYCLOPÆDIA BRITANNICA.

GOVERNMENT.

I.

The End of Government; viz. the Good or Benefit for the Sake of which it exists.

THE question with respect to Government is a question about the adaptation of means to an end. Notwithstanding the portion of discourse which has been bestowed upon this subject, it is surprising to find, on a close inspection, how few of its principles are settled. The reason is, that the ends and means have not been analyzed; and it is only a general and undistinguishing conception of them, which is found in the minds of the greatest number of men. Things, in this situation, give rise to interminable disputes; more especially when the deliberation is subject, as here, to the strongest action of personal interest.

In a discourse, limited as the present, it would be obviously vain to attempt the accomplishment of such a task as that of the analysis we have mentioned. The mode, however, in which the operation should be conducted, may perhaps be described, and evidence enough exhibited to shew in what road we must travel, to approach the goal at which so many have vainly endeavoured to arrive.

The end of Government has been described in a great variety of expressions. By Locke it was said to be "the public good;" by others it has been described as being "the greatest happiness of the greatest number." These, and equivalent expressions, are just; but they are defective, inasmuch as the particular ideas which they embrace are indistinctly announced; and different conceptions are by means of them raised in different minds, and even in the same mind on different occasions.

It is immediately obvious, that a wide and difficult field is presented, and that the whole science of human nature must be explored, to lay a foundation for the science of Government.

To understand what is included in the happiness of the greatest number, we must understand what is included in the happiness of the individuals of whom it is composed.

That dissection of human nature which would be necessary for exhibiting, on proper evidence, the primary elements into which human happiness may be resolved, it is not compatible with the present design to undertake. We must content ourselves with assuming certain results.

We may allow, for example, in general terms, that the lot of every human being is determined by his pains and pleasures; and that his happiness corresponds with the degree in which his pleasures are great, and his pains are small.

Human pains and pleasures are derived from two sources:—They are produced, either by our fellow-men, or by causes independent of other men.

We may assume it as another principle, that the concern of Government is with the former of these two sources; that its business is to increase to the utmost the pleasures, and diminish to the utmost the pains, which men derive from one another.

Of the laws of nature, on which the condition of man depends, that which is attended with the greatest number of consequences, is the necessity of labour for obtaining the means of subsistence, as well as the means of the greatest part of our pleasures. This is, no doubt, the primary cause of Government; for, if nature had produced spontaneously all the objects which we desire, and in sufficient abundance for the desires of all, there would have been no source of dispute or of injury among men; nor would any man have possessed the means of ever acquiring authority over another.

The results are exceedingly different, when nature produces the objects of desire not in sufficient abundance for all. The source of dispute is then exhaustless; and every man has the means of acquiring authority over others, in proportion to the quantity of those objects which he is able to possess.

In this case, the end to be obtained, through Government as the means, is, to make that distribution of the scanty materials of happiness, which would insure the greatest sum of it in the members of the community, taken altogether, preventing every individual, or combination of individuals, from interfering with that distribution, or making any man to have less than his share.

When it is considered that most of the objects of desire, and even the means of subsistence, are the product of labour, it is evident that the means of insuring labour must be provided for as the foundation of all.

The means for the insuring of labour are of two sorts; the one made out of the matter of evil, the other made out of the matter of good.

The first sort is commonly denominated force; and, under its application, the labourers are slaves. This mode of procuring labour we need not consider; for, if the end of Government be to produce the greatest happiness of the greatest number, that end cannot be attained by making the greatest number slaves.

The other mode of obtaining labour is by allurement, or the advantage which it brings. To obtain all the objects of desire in the greatest possible quantity, we must obtain labour in the greatest possible quantity; and, to obtain labour in the greatest possible quantity, we must raise to the greatest possible height the advantage attached to labour. It is impossible to attach to labour a greater degree of advantage than the whole of the product of labour. Why so? Because, if you give more to one man than the produce of his labour, you can do so only by taking it away from the produce of some other man's labour. The greatest possible happiness of society is, therefore, attained by insuring to every man the greatest possible quantity of the produce of his labour.

How is this to be accomplished? for it is obvious that every man, who has not all the objects of his desire, has inducement to take them from any other man who is weaker than himself: and how is he to be prevented?

One mode is sufficiently obvious; and it does not appear that there is any other: The union of a certain number of men, to protect one another. The object, it is plain, can best be attained when a great number of men combine, and delegate to a small number the power necessary for protecting them all. This is Government.

With respect to the end of Government, or that for the sake of which it exists, it is not conceived to be necessary, on the present occasion, that the analysis should be carried any further. What follows is an attempt to analyze the means.

II.

The Means of attaining the End of Government; viz. Power, and Securities against the Abuse of that Power.

Two things are here to be considered; the power with which the small number are entrusted; and the use which they are to make of it.

With respect to the first, there is no difficulty. The elements, out of which the power of coercing others is fabricated, are obvious to all. Of these we shall, therefore, not lengthen this article by any explanation.

All the difficult questions of Government relate to the means of restraining those, in whose hands are lodged the powers necessary for the protection of all, from making a bad use of it.

Whatever would be the temptations under which individuals would lie, if there was no Government, to take the objects of desire from others weaker than themselves, under the same temptations the members of Government lie, to take the objects of desire from the members of the community, if they are not prevented from doing so. Whatever, then, are the reasons for establishing Government, the very same exactly are the reasons for establishing securities, that those entrusted with the powers necessary for protecting others make use of them for that purpose solely, and not for the purpose of taking from the members of the community the objects of desire.

III.

That the requisite Securities against the Abuse of Power, are not found in any of the simple Forms of Government.

There are three modes in which it may be supposed that the powers for the protection of the community are capable of being exercised. The community may undertake the protection of itself, and of its members. The powers of protection may be placed in the hands of a few. And, lastly, they may be placed in the hands of an individual. The Many, The Few, The One; These varieties appear to exhaust the subject. It is not possible to conceive any hands, or combination of hands, in which the powers of protection can be lodged, which will not fall under one or other of those descriptions. And these varieties correspond to the three forms of Government, the Democratical, the Aristocratical, and the Monarchical.

It will be necessary to look somewhat closely at each of these forms in their order.

1. THE DEMOCRATICAL.—It is obviously impossible that the community in a body can be present to afford protection to each of its members. It must employ individuals for that purpose. Employing individuals, it must choose them; it must lay down the rules under which they are to act; and it must punish them, if they act in disconformity to those rules. In these functions are included the three great operations of Government—Administration, Legislation, and Judicature. The community, to perform any of these operations, must be assembled. This circumstance alone seems to form a conclusive objection against the democratical form. To assemble the whole of a community as often as the business of Government requires performance would almost preclude the existence of labour; hence that of property; and hence the existence of the community itself.

There is another objection, not less conclusive. A whole community would form a numerous assembly. But all numerous assemblies are essentially incapable of business. It is unnecessary to be tedious in the proof of this proposition. In an assembly, every thing must be done by speaking and assenting. But where the assembly is numerous, so many persons desire to speak, and feelings, by mutual inflammation, become so violent, that calm and effectual deliberation is impossible.

It may be taken, therefore, as a position, from which there will be no dissent, that a community in mass is ill adapted for the business of Government. There is no principle more in conformity with the sentiments and the practice of the people than this. The management of the joint affairs of any considerable body of the people they never undertake for themselves. What they uniformly do is, to choose a certain number of themselves to be the actors in their stead. Even in the case of a common Benefit Club, the members choose a Committee of Management, and content themselves with a general controul.

2. THE ARISTOCRATICAL.—This term applies to all those cases, in which the powers of Government are held by any number of persons

intermediate between a single person and the majority. When the number is small, it is common to call the Government an Oligarchy; when it is considerable, to call it an Aristocracy. The cases are essentially the same; because the motives which operate in both are the same. This is a proposition which carries, we think, its own evidence along with it. We, therefore, assume it as a point which will not be disputed.

The source of evil is radically different, in the case of Aristocracy, from what it is in that of Democracy.

The Community cannot have an interest opposite to its interest. To affirm this would be a contradiction in terms. The Community within itself, and with respect to itself, can have no sinister interest. One Community may intend the evil of another; never its own. This is an indubitable proposition, and one of great importance. The Community may act wrong from mistake. To suppose that it could from design, would be to suppose that human beings can wish their own misery.

The circumstances, from which the inaptitude of the community, as a body, for the business of Government, arises, namely, the inconvenience of assembling them, and the inconvenience of their numbers when assembled, do not necessarily exist in the case of Aristocracy. If the number of those who hold among them the powers of Government is so great, as to make it inconvenient to assemble them, or impossible for them to deliberate calmly when assembled, this is only an objection to so extended an Aristocracy, and has no application to an Aristocracy not too numerous, when assembled, for the best exercise of deliberation.

The question is, whether such an Aristrocracy may be trusted to make that use of the powers of Government which is most conducive to the end for which Government exists?

There may be a strong presumption that any Aristocracy, monopolizing the powers of Government, would not possess intellectual powers in any very high perfection. Intellectual powers are the offspring of labour. But an hereditary Aristrocracy are deprived of the strongest motives to labour. The greater part of them will, therefore, be defective in those mental powers. This is one objection, and an important one, though not the greatest.

We have already observed, that the reason for which Government exists is, that one man, if stronger than another, will take from him whatever that other possesses and he desires. But if one man will do this, so will several. And if powers are put into the hands of a comparatively small number, called an Aristocracy, powers which make them stronger than the rest of the community, they will take from the rest of the community as much as they please of the objects of desire. They will, thus, defeat the very end for which Government was instituted. The unfitness, therefore, of an Aristocracy to be entrusted with the powers of Government, rests on demonstration.

3. THE MONARCHICAL.—It will be seen, and therefore words to make it manifest are unnecessary, that, in most respects, the Monarchical form

of Government agrees with the Aristocratical, and is liable to the same objections.

If Government is founded upon this, as a law of human nature, that a man, if able, will take from others any thing which they have and he desires, it is sufficiently evident that when a man is called a King, it does not change his nature; so that when he has got power to enable him to take from every man what he pleases, he will take whatever he pleases. To suppose that he will not, is to affirm that Government is unnecessary; and that human beings will abstain from injuring one another of their own accord.

It is very evident that this reasoning extends to every modification of the smaller number. Whenever the powers of Government are placed in any hands other than those of the community, whether those of one man, of a few, or of several, those principles of human nature which imply that Government is at all necessary, imply that those persons will make use of them to defeat the very end for which Government exists.

IV.
An Objection stated — and answered.

One observation, however, suggests itself. Allowing, it may be said, that this deduction is perfect, and the inference founded upon it indisputable, it is yet true, that if there were no Government, every man would be exposed to depredation from every man; but, under an Aristocracy, he is exposed to it only from a few; under a Monarchy, only from one.

This is a highly-important objection, and deserves to be minutely investigated.

It is sufficiently obvious, that, if every man is liable to be deprived of what he possesses at the will of every man stronger than himself, the existence of property is impossible; and, if the existence of property is impossible, so also is that of labour, of the means of subsistence for an enlarged community, and hence of the community itself. If the members of such a community are liable to deprivation by only a few hundred men, the members of an Aristocracy, it may not be impossible to satiate that limited number with a limited portion of the objects belonging to all. Allowing this view of the subject to be correct, it follows, that the smaller the number of hands into which the powers of Government are permitted to pass, the happier it will be for the community: that an Oligarchy, therefore, is better than an Aristocracy, and a Monarchy better than either.

This view of the subject deserves to be the more carefully considered, because the conclusion to which it leads is the same with that which has been adopted and promulgated, by some of the most profound and most benevolent investigators of human affairs. That Government by one man, altogether unlimited and uncontrolled, is better than Government by any modification of Aristocracy, is the celebrated opinion of Mr. Hobbes, and of the French *Economists*, supported on reasonings which it is not easy to controvert. Government by the many, they with reason considered an impossibility. They inferred, therefore, that, of all the possible forms of Government, absolute Monarchy is the best.

Experience, if we look only at the outside of the facts, appears to be divided on this subject. Absolute Monarchy, under Neros and Caligulas, under such men as Emperors of Morocco and Sultans of Turkey, is the scourge of human nature. On the other side, the people of Denmark, tired out with the oppression of an Aristocracy, resolved that their King should be absolute, and, under their absolute Monarch, are as well governed as any people in Europe. In Greece, notwithstanding the defects of Democracy, human nature ran a more brilliant career than it has ever done in any other age or country.

As the surface of history affords, therefore, no certain principle of decision, we must go beyond the surface, and penetrate to the springs within.

When it is said that one man, or a limited number of men, will soon be satiated with the objects of desire, and, when they have taken from the community what suffices to satiate them, will protect its members in the enjoyment of the remainder, an important element of the calculation is left out. Human beings are not a passive substance. If human beings, in respect to their rulers, were the same as sheep in respect to their shepherd; and if the King, or the Aristocracy, were as totally exempt from all fear of resistance from the people, and all chance of obtaining more obedience from severity, as the shepherd in the case of the sheep, it does appear that there would be a limit to the motive for taking to one's self the objects of desire. The case will be found to be very much altered when the idea is taken into the account, first, of the resistance to his will which one human being may expect from another; and secondly, of that perfection in obedience which fear alone can produce.

That one human being will desire to render the person and property of another subservient to his pleasures, notwithstanding the pain or loss of pleasure which it may occasion to that other individual, is the foundation of Government. The desire of the object implies the desire of the power necessary to accomplish the object. The desire, therefore, of that power which is necessary to render the persons and properties of human beings subservient to our pleasures, is a grand governing law of human nature.

What is implied in that desire of power; and what is the extent to which it carries the actions of men; are the questions which it is necessary to resolve, in order to discover the limit which nature has set to the desire on the part of a King, or an Aristocracy, to inflict evil upon the community for their own advantage.

Power is a means to an end. The end is every thing, without exception, which the human being calls pleasure, and the removal of pain. The grand instrument for attaining what a man likes is the actions of other men. Power, in its most appropriate signification, therefore, means security for the conformity between the will of one man and the acts of other men. This, we presume, is not a proposition which will be disputed. The master has power over his servant, because when he wills him to do so and so,—in other words, expresses a desire that he would do so and so, he possesses a kind of security that the actions of the man will correspond to his desire. The General commands his soldiers to perform certain operations, the King commands his subjects to act in a certain manner, and their power is complete or not complete, in proportion as the conformity is complete or not complete between the actions willed and the actions performed. The actions of other men, considered as means for the attainment of the objects of our desire, are perfect or imperfect, in proportion as they are or are not certainly and invariably correspondent to our will. There is no limit, therefore, to the demand of security for the perfection of that correspondence. A man is never satisfied with a smaller degree if he can obtain a greater. And as there is no man whatsoever, whose acts, in some degree or other, in some way or other, more immediately or more remotely, may not have some influence as means to our ends, there is no man, the conformity of whose acts to our will we would not give something to secure. The demand, therefore, of power over the acts of other men is really boundless. It is boundless in two ways; boundless in the number of persons to whom we would extend it, and boundless in its degree over the actions of each.

It would be nugatory to say, with a view to explain away this important principle, that some human beings may be so remotely connected with our interests as to make the desire of a conformity between our will and their actions evanescent. It is quite enough to assume, what nobody will deny, that our desire of that conformity is unlimited, in respect to all those men whose actions can be supposed to have any influence on our pains and pleasures. With respect to the rulers of a community, this at least is certain, that they have a desire for the uniformity between their will and the actions of every man in the community. And for our present purpose, this is as wide a field as we need to embrace.

With respect to the community, then, we deem it an established truth, that the rulers, one or a few, desire an exact conformity between their will and the acts of every member of the community. It remains for us to inquire to what description of acts it is the nature of this desire to give existence.

There are two classes of means by which the conformity between the will of one man and the acts of other men may be accomplished. The one is pleasure, the other pain.

With regard to securities of the pleasurable sort for obtaining a conformity between one man's will and the acts of other men, it is evident, from experience, that when a man possesses a command over the objects of desire, he may, by imparting those objects to other men, insure, to a great extent, conformity between his will and their actions. It follows, and is also matter of experience, that the greater the quantity of the objects of desire, which he may thus impart to other men, the greater is the number of men between whose actions and his own will he can insure a conformity. As it has been demonstrated that there is no limit to the number of men whose actions we desire to have conformable to our will, it follows, with equal evidence, that there is no limit to the command which we desire to possess over the objects which ensure this result.

It is, therefore, not true, that there is in the mind of a King, or in the minds of an Aristocracy, any point of saturation with the objects of desire. The opinion, in examination of which we have gone through the preceding analysis, that a King or an Aristocracy may be satiated with the objects of desire, and, after being satiated, leave to the members of the community the greater part of what belongs to them, is an opinion founded upon a partial and incomplete view of the laws of human nature.

We have next to consider the securities of the painful sort which may be employed for attaining conformity between the acts of one man and the will of another.

We are of opinion, that the importance of this part of the subject has not been duly considered; and that the business of Government will be ill understood, till its numerous consequences have been fully developed.

Pleasure appears to be a feeble instrument of obedience in comparison with pain. It is much more easy to despise pleasure than pain. Above all, it is important to consider, that in this class of instruments is included the power of taking away life, and with it of taking away not only all the pleasures of reality, but, what goes so far beyond them, all the pleasures of hope. This class of securities is, therefore, incomparably the strongest. He who desires obedience, to a high degree of exactness, cannot be satisfied with the power of giving pleasure, he must have the power of inflicting pain. He who desires it, to the highest possible degree of exactness, must desire power of inflicting pain sufficient at least to insure that degree of exactness; that is, an unlimited power of inflicting pain; for, as there is no possible mark by which to distinguish what is sufficient and what is not, and as the human mind sets no bounds to its avidity for the securities of what it deems eminently good, it is sure to extend, beyond almost any limits, its desire of the power of giving pain to others.

It may, however, be said, that how inseparable a part soever of human nature it may appear to be, to desire to possess unlimited power of inflicting pain upon others, it does not follow, that those who possess it will have a desire to make use of it.

This is the next part of the inquiry upon which we have to enter; and we need not add that it merits all the attention of those who would possess correct ideas upon a subject which involves the greatest interests of mankind.

The chain of inference, in this case, is close and strong, to a most unusual degree. A man desires that the actions of other men shall be instantly and accurately correspondent to his will. He desires that the actions of the greatest possible number shall be so. Terror is the grand instrument. Terror can work only through assurance that evil will follow any want of conformity between the will and the actions willed. Every failure must, therefore, be punished. As there are no bounds to the mind's desire of its pleasure, there are of course no bounds to its desire of perfection in the instruments of that pleasure. There are, therefore, no bounds to its desire of exactness in the conformity between its will and the actions willed; and, by consequence, to the strength of that terror which is its procuring cause. Every, the most minute, failure, must be visited with the heaviest infliction: and, as failure in extreme exactness must frequently happen, the occasions of cruelty must be incessant.

We have thus arrived at several conclusions of the highest possible importance. We have seen, that the very principle of human nature upon which the necessity of Government is founded, the propensity of one man to possess himself of the objects of desire at the cost of another, leads on, by infallible sequence, where power over a community is attained, and nothing checks, not only to that degree of plunder which leaves the members (excepting always the recipients and instruments of the plunder) the bare means of subsistence, but to that degree of cruelty which is necessary to keep in existence the most intense terror.

The world affords some decisive experiments upon human nature, in exact conformity with these conclusions. An English Gentleman may be taken as a favourable specimen of civilization, of knowledge, of humanity, of all the qualities, in short, that make human nature estimable. The degree in which he desires to possess power over his fellow-creatures, and the degree of oppression to which he finds motives for carrying the exercise of that power, will afford a standard from which, assuredly, there can be no appeal. Wherever the same motives exist, the same conduct, as that displayed by the English Gentleman, may be expected to follow, in all men not farther advanced in human excellence than him. In the West Indies, before that vigilant attention of the English nation, which now, for thirty years, has imposed so great a check upon the masters of slaves, there was not a perfect absence of all check upon the dreadful propensities of power. But yet it is true, that these propensities led English Gentlemen, not only to deprive their slaves of property, and to make property of their fellow-creatures, but to treat them with a degree of cruelty, the very description of which froze the blood of their countrymen, who were placed in less unfavourable circumstances. The motives of this deplorable conduct are exactly those which we have described above, as arising out of the universal desire to render the actions of other men exactly conformable to our will. It is of great importance to remark, that not one item in the motives which had led English Gentlemen to make slaves of their fellow-creatures, and to reduce them to the very worst condition in which the negroes have been found in the West Indies, can be shown to be wanting, or to be less strong in the set of motives, which universally operate upon the men who have power over their fellow-creatures. It is proved, therefore, by the closest deduction from the acknowledged laws of human nature, and by direct and decisive experiments, that the ruling One, or the ruling Few, would, if checks did not operate in the way of prevention, reduce the great mass of the people subject to their power, at least to the condition of negroes in the West Indies.*

We have thus seen, that of the forms of Government, which have been called the three simple forms, not one is adequate to the ends which Government is appointed to secure; that the community itself, which alone is free from motives opposite to those ends, is incapacitated by its numbers from performing the business of Government; and that whether Government is intrusted to one or a few, they have not only motives opposite to those ends, but motives which will carry them, if unchecked, to inflict the greatest evils.

These conclusions are so conformable to ordinary conceptions, that it would hardly have been necessary, if the development had not been of importance for some of our subsequent investigations, to have taken any pains with the proof of them. In this country, at least, it will be remarked, in conformity with so many writers, that the imperfection of the three simple forms of Government is apparent; that the ends of Government can be attained in perfection only, as under the British Constitution, by an union of all the three.

V.

That the requisite Securities are not found in a Union of the Three simple Forms of Government; — Doctrine of the Constitutional Balance.

The doctrine of the union of the three simple forms of Government is the next part of this important subject which we are called upon to examine.

The first thing which it is obvious to remark upon it, is, that it has been customary, in regard to this part of the inquiry, to beg the question. The good effects which have been ascribed to the union of the three simple forms of Government, have been *supposed*; and the supposition has commonly been allowed. No proof has been adduced; or if any thing have the appearance of proof, it has only been a reference to the British Constitution. The British Constitution, it has been said, is an union of the three simple forms of Government; and the British Government is excellent. To render the instance of the British Government in any degree a proof of the doctrine in question, it is evident that three points must be established; 1st, That the British Government is not in show,

---

* An acute sense of this important truth is expressed by the President Montesquieu: " C'est une experience eternelle, que tout homme qui a du pouvoir est porte a en abuser; il va jusqu'a ce qu'il trouve de limites."—*Esp. de Loix*, II. 4.

but in substance, an union of the three simple forms; 2dly, That it has peculiar excellence; and, 3dly, That its excellence arises from the union so supposed, and not from any other cause. As these points have always been taken for granted without examination, the question with respect to the effects of an union of the three simple forms of Government may be considered as yet unsolved.

The positions which we have already established with regard to human nature, and which we assume as foundations, are these: That the actions of men are governed by their wills, and their wills by their desires: That their desires are directed to pleasure and relief from pain as *ends*, and to wealth and power as the principal means: That to the desire of these means there is no limit; and that the actions which flow from this unlimited desire are the constituents whereof bad Government is made. Reasoning correctly from these acknowledged laws of human nature, we shall presently discover what opinion, with respect to the mixture of the different species of Government, it will be incumbent upon us to adopt.

The theory in question implies, that of the powers of Government, one portion is held by the King, one by the Aristocracy, and one by the people. It also implies, that there is on the part of each of them a certain unity of will, otherwise they would not act as three separate powers. This being understood, we proceed to the inquiry.

From the principles which we have already laid down, it follows, That of the objects of human desire—and, speaking more definitely, of the means to the ends of human desire, namely, wealth and power—each of the three parties will endeavour to obtain as much as possible.

After what has been said, it is not suspected that any reader will deny this proposition; but it is of importance that he keep in his mind a very clear conception of it.

If any expedient presents itself to any of the supposed parties, effectual to said end, and not opposed to any preferred object of pursuit, we may infer, with certainty, that it will be adopted. One effectual expedient is not more effectual than obvious. Any two of the parties, by combining, may swallow up the third. That such combination will take place, appears to be as certain as any thing which depends upon human will; because there are strong motives in favour of it, and none that can be conceived in opposition to it. Whether the portions of power, as originally distributed to the parties, be supposed to be equal or unequal, the mixture of three of the kinds of Government, it is thus evident, cannot possibly exist.

This proposition appears to be so perfectly proved, that we do not think it necessary to dwell here upon the subject. As a part, however, of this doctrine, of the mixture of the simple forms of Government, it may be proper to inquire, whether an union may not be possible of two of them.

Three varieties of this union may be conceived; the union of the Monarchy with Aristocracy, or the union of either with Democracy.

Let us first suppose that Monarchy is united with Aristocracy. Their power is equal or not equal. If it is not equal, it follows, as a necessary consequence, from the principles which we have already established, that the stronger will take from the weaker, till it engrosses the whole. The only question, therefore, is, What will happen when the power is equal.

In the first place, it seems impossible that such equality should ever exist. How is it to be established? Or by what criterion is it to be ascertained? If there is no such criterion, it must, in all cases, be the result of chance. If so, the chances against it are as infinite to one. The idea, therefore, is wholly chimerical and absurd.

Besides, A disposition to overrate one's own advantages, and underrate those of other men, is a known law of human nature. Suppose, what would be little less than miraculous, that equality were established, this propensity would lead each of the parties to conceive itself the strongest. The consequence would be that they would go to war, and contend till one or other was subdued. Either those laws of human nature, upon which all reasoning with respect to Government proceeds, must be denied, and then the utility of Government itself may be denied, or this conclusion is demonstrated. Again, if this equality were established, is there a human being who can suppose that it would last? If any thing be known about human affairs it is this, that they are in perpetual change. If nothing else interfered, the difference of men in respect of talents, would abundantly produce the effect. Suppose your equality to be established at the time when your King is a man of talents, and suppose his successor to be the reverse; your equality no longer exists. The moment one of the parties is superior, it begins to profit by its superiority, and the inequality is daily increased. It is unnecessary to extend the investigation to the remaining cases, the union of democracy with either of the other two kinds of Government. It is very evident that the same reasoning would lead to the same results.

In this doctrine of the mixture of the simple forms of Government, is included the celebrated theory of the Balance among the component parts of a Government. By this, it is supposed, that, when a Government is composed of Monarchy, Aristocracy, and Democracy, they balance one another, and by mutual checks produce good government. A few words will suffice to show, that, if any theory deserve the epithets of " wild, visionary, chimerical," it is that of the Balance. If there are three powers, how is it possible to prevent two of them from combining to swallow up the third?

The analysis which we have already performed, will enable us to trace rapidly the concatenation of causes and effects in this imagined case.

We have already seen that the interest of the community, considered in the aggregate, or in the democratical point of view, is, that each individual should receive protection, and that the powers which are constituted for that purpose should be employed exclusively for that purpose. As this is a proposition wholly indisputable, it is also one to which all correct reasoning upon matters of Government must have a perpetual reference.

We have also seen that the interest of the King, and of the governing Aristocracy, is directly the reverse; it is to have unlimited power over the rest of the community, and to use it for their own advantage. In the supposed case of the balance of the Monarchical, Aristocratical, and Democratical powers, it cannot be for the interest of either the Monarchy or the Aristocracy to combine with the Democracy; because it is the interest of the Democracy, or community at large, that neither the King nor the Aristocracy should have one particle of power, or one particle of the wealth of the community, for their own advantage.

The Democracy or Community have all possible motives to endeavour to prevent the Monarchy and Aristocracy from exercising power, or obtaining the wealth of the community, for their own advantage: The Monarchy and Aristocracy have all possible motives for endeavouring to obtain unlimited power over the persons and property of the community: The consequence is inevitable; they have all possible motives for combining to obtain that power, and unless the people have power enough to be a match for both, they have no protection. The balance, therefore, is a thing, the existence of which, upon the best possible evidence, is to be regarded as impossible. The appearances which have given colour to the supposition are altogether delusive.

VI.

In the Representative System alone the Securities for good Government are to be found.

What then is to be done? For, according to this reasoning, we may be told that good Government appears to be impossible. The people, as a body, cannot perform the business of Government for themselves. If the powers of Government are entrusted to one man, or a few men, and a Monarchy, or governing Aristocracy, is formed, the results are fatal: And it appears that a combination of the simple forms is impossible.

Notwithstanding the truth of these propositions, it is not yet proved that good Government is impossible. For though the people, who cannot exercise the powers of Government themselves, must entrust them to some one individual or set of individuals, and such individuals will infallibly have the strongest motives to make a bad use of them, it is possible that checks may be found sufficient to prevent them. The next subject of inquiry, then, is the doctrine of checks. It is sufficiently conformable to the established and fashionable opinions to say, that, upon the right constitution of checks, all goodness of Government depends. To this proposition we fully subscribe. Nothing, therefore, can exceed the importance of correct conclusions upon this subject. After the developements already made, it is hoped that the inquiry will be neither intricate nor unsatisfactory.

In the grand discovery of modern times, the system of representation, the solution of all the difficulties, both speculative and practical, will perhaps be found. If it cannot, we seem to be forced upon the extraordinary conclusion, that good Government is impossible. For as there is no individual, or combination of individuals, except the community itself, who would not have an interest in bad Government, if entrusted with its powers ; and as the community itself is incapable of exercising those powers, and must entrust them to some individual or combination of individuals, the conclusion is obvious : The Community itself must check those individuals, else they will follow their interest, and produce bad Government.

But how is it the Community can check ? The community can act only when assembled: And then it is incapable of acting.

The community, however, can chuse Representatives: And the question is, whether the Representatives of the Community can operate as a check?

VII.

What is required in a Representative Body to make it a Security for good Government?

We may begin by laying down two propositions, which appear to involve a great portion of the inquiry ; and about which it is unlikely that there will be any dispute.

I. The checking body must have a degree of power sufficient for the business of checking.

II. It must have an identity of interest with the community ; otherwise it will make a mischievous use of its power.

I. To measure the degree of power which is requisite upon any occasion, we must consider the degree of power which is necessary to be overcome. Just as much as suffices for that purpose is requisite, and no more. We have then to inquire what power it is which the Representatives of the community, acting as a check, need power to overcome. The answer here is easily given. It is all that power, wheresoever lodged, which they, in whose hands it is lodged, have an interest in misusing. We have already seen, that to whomsoever the community entrusts the powers of Government, whether one, or a few, they have an interest in misusing them. All the power, therefore, which the one or the few, or which the one and the few combined, can apply to insure the accomplishment of their sinister ends, the checking body must have power to overcome, otherwise its check will be unavailing. In other words, there will be no check.

This is so exceedingly evident, that we hardly think it necessary to say another word in illustration of it. If a King is prompted by the inherent principles of human nature to seek the gratification of his will; and if he finds an obstacle in that pursuit, he removes it, of course, if he can. If any man, or any set of men, oppose him, he overcomes them, if he is able ; and to prevent him, they must, at the least, have equal power with himself.

The same is the case with an Aristocracy. To oppose them with success in pursuing their interest at the expense of the community, the checking body must have power successfully to resist whatever power they possess. If there is both a King and an Aristocracy, and if they would combine to put down the checking force, and to pursue their mutual interest at the expense of the community, the checking body must have sufficient power successfully to resist the united power of both King and Aristocracy.

These conclusions are not only indisputable, but the very theory of the British Constitution is erected upon them. The House of Commons, according to that theory, is the checking body. It is also an admitted doctrine, that if the King had the power of bearing down any opposition to his will that could be made by the House of Commons; or if the King and the House of Lords combined had the power of bearing down its opposition to their joint will, it would cease to have the power of checking them; it must, therefore, have a power sufficient to overcome the united power of both.

II. All the questions which relate to the degree of power necessary to be given to that checking body, on the perfection of whose operations all the goodness of Government depends, are thus pretty easily solved. The grand difficulty consists in finding the means of constituting a checking body, whose powers shall not be turned against the community for whose protection it is created.

There can be no doubt, that if power is granted to a body of men, called Representatives, they, like any other men, will use their power, not for the advantage of the community, but for their own advantage, if they can. The only question is, therefore, how they can be prevented? in other words, how are the interests of the Representatives to be identified with those of the community?

Each Representative may be considered in two capacities; in his capacity of Representative, in which he has the exercise of power over others, and in his capacity of Member of the Community, in which others have the exercise of power over him.

If things were so arranged, that, in his capacity of Representative, it would be impossible for him to do himself so much good by misgovernment, as he would do himself harm in his capacity of member of the community, the object would be accomplished. We have already seen, that the amount of power assigned to the checking body cannot be diminished beyond a certain amount. It must be sufficient to overcome all resistance on the part of all those in whose hands the powers of Government are lodged. But if the power assigned to the Representative cannot be diminished in amount, there is only one other way in which it can be diminished, and that is, in duration.

This, then, is the instrument; lessening of duration is the instrument, by which, if by any thing, the object is to be attained. The smaller the period of time during which any man retains his capacity of Representative, as compared with the time in which he is simply a member of the community, the more difficult it will be to compensate the sacrifice of the interests of the longer period, by the profits of misgovernment during the shorter.

This is an old and approved method of identifying as nearly as possible the interests of those who rule with the interests of those who are ruled. It is in pursuance of this advantage, that the Members of the

British House of Commons have always been chosen for a limited period. If the Members were hereditary, or even if they were chosen for life, every inquirer would immediately pronounce that they would employ, for their own advantage, the powers entrusted to them; and that they would go just as far in abusing the persons and properties of the people, as their estimate of the powers and spirit of the people to resist them would allow them to contemplate as safe.

As it thus appears, by the consent of all men, from the time when the Romans made their Consuls annual, down to the present day, that the end is to be attained by limiting the duration, either of the acting, or (which is better) of the checking power, the next question is, to what degree should the limitation proceed?

The general answer is plain. It should proceed, till met by overbalancing inconveniences on the other side. What then are the inconveniences which are likely to flow from a too limited duration?

They are of two sorts; those which affect the performance of the service, for which the individuals are chosen, and those which arise from the trouble of election. It is sufficiently obvious, that the business of Government requires time to perform it. The matter must be proposed, deliberated upon, a resolution must be taken, and executed. If the powers of Government were to be shifted from one set of hands to another every day, the business of Government could not proceed. Two conclusions, then, we may adopt with perfect certainty; that whatsoever time is necessary to perform the periodical round of the stated operations of Government, this should be allotted to those who are invested with the checking powers; and secondly, that no time, which is not necessary for that purpose, should by any means be allotted to them. With respect to the inconvenience arising from frequency of election, though, it is evident, that the trouble of election, which is always something, should not be repeated oftener than is necessary, no great allowance will need to be made for it, because it may easily be reduced to an inconsiderable amount.

As it thus appears, that limiting the duration of their power is a security against the sinister interest of the people's Representatives, so it appears that it is the only security of which the nature of the case admits. The only other means which could be employed to that end, would be punishment on account of abuse. It is easy, however, to see, that punishment could not be effectually applied. In order for punishment, definition is required of the punishable acts; and proof must be established of the commission. But abuses of power may be carried to a great extent, without allowing the means of proving a determinate offence. No part of political experience is more perfect than this.

If the limiting of duration be the only security, it is unnecessary to speak of the importance which ought to be attached to it.

In the principle of limiting the duration of the power delegated to the Representatives of the people, is not included the idea of changing them. The same individual may be chosen any number of times. The check of the short period, for which he is chosen, and during which he can promote his sinister interest, is the same upon the man who has been chosen and re-chosen twenty times, as upon the man who has been chosen for the first time. And there is good reason for always re-electing the man who has done his duty, because the longer he serves, the better acquainted he becomes with the business of the service. Upon this principle of rechoosing, or of the permanency of the individual, united with the power of change, has been recommended the plan of permanent service with perpetual power of removal. This, it has been said, reduces the period within which the Representative can promote his sinister interest to the narrowest possible limits; because the moment when his Constituents begin to suspect him, that moment they may turn him out. On the other hand, if he continues faithful, the trouble of election is performed once for all, and the man serves as long as he lives. Some disadvantages, on the other hand, would accompany this plan. The present, however, is not the occasion on which the balance of different plans is capable of being compared.

VIII.

What is required in the Elective Body to secure the requisite Properties in the Representative Body.

Having considered the means which are capable of being employed for identifying the interest of the Representatives, when chosen, with that of the persons who choose them, it remains that we endeavour to bring to view the principles which ought to guide in determining who the persons are by whom the act of choosing ought to be performed.

It is most evident, that, upon this question, every thing depends. It can be of no consequence to insure, by shortness of duration, a conformity between the conduct of the Representatives and the will of those who appoint them, if those who appoint them have an interest opposite to that of the community; because those who choose will, according to the principles of human nature, make choice of such persons as will act according to their wishes. As this is a direct inference from the very principle on which Government itself is founded, we assume it as indisputable.

We have seen already, that if one man has power over others placed in his hands, he will make use of it for an evil purpose; for the purpose of rendering those other men the abject instruments of his will. If we, then, suppose, that one man has the power of choosing the Representatives of the people, it follows, that he will choose men who will use their power as Representatives for the promotion of this his sinister interest.

We have likewise seen, that when a few men have power given them over others, they will make use of it exactly for the same ends, and to the same extent, as the one man. It equally follows, that, if a small number of men have the choice of the Representatives, such Representatives will be chosen as will promote the interests of that small number, by reducing, if possible, the rest of the community to be the abject and helpless slaves of their will.

In all these cases, it is obvious and indisputable, that all the benefits of the Representative system are lost. The Representative system is, in that case, only an operose and clumsy machinery for doing that which might as well be done without it; reducing the community to subjection, under the One, or the Few.

When we say the Few, it is seen that, in this case, it is of no importance whether we mean a few hundreds, or a few thousands, or even many thousands. The operation of the sinister interest is the same; and the fate is the same of all that part of the community over whom the power is exercised. A numerous Aristocracy has never been found to be less oppressive than an Aristocracy confined to a few.

The general conclusion, therefore, which is evidently established is this; that the benefits of the Representative system are lost, in all cases in which the interests of the choosing body are not the same with those of the community.

It is very evident, that if the community itself were the choosing body, the interest of the community and that of the choosing body would be the same. The question is, whether that of any portion of the community, if erected into the choosing body, would remain the same?

One thing is pretty clear, that all those individuals whose interests are indisputably included in those of other individuals, may be struck off without inconvenience. In this light may be viewed all children, up to a certain age, whose interests are involved in those of their parents. In this light, also, women may be regarded, the interest of almost all of whom is involved either in that of their fathers or in that of their husbands.

Having ascertained that an interest identical with that of the whole community, is to be found in the aggregate males, of an age to be regarded as *sui juris*, who may be regarded as the natural Representatives of the whole population, we have to go on, and inquire, whether this requisite quality may not be found in some less number, some aliquot part of that body.

As degrees of mental qualities are not easily ascertained, outward and visible signs must be taken to distinguish, for this purpose, one part of these males from another. Applicable signs of this description appear to be three; Years, Property, Profession or Mode of Life.

According to the first of these means of distinction, a portion of the males, to any degree limited, may be taken, by prescribing an advanced period of life at which the power of voting for a Representative should commence. According to the second, the elective body may be limited, by allowing a vote to those only who possess a certain amount of property or of income. According to the third, they may be limited, by allowing a vote only to such persons as belong to certain professions, or certain connexions and interests. What we have to inquire is, if the interest of the number, limited and set apart, upon any of those principles, as the organ of choice for a body of Representatives, will be the same with the interest of the community?

With respect to the first principle of selection, that of age, it would appear that a considerable latitude may be taken without inconvenience. Suppose the age of forty were prescribed, as that at which the right of Suffrage should commence; scarcely any laws could be made for the benefit of all the men of forty which would not be laws for the benefit of all the rest of the community.

The great principle of security here is, that the men of forty have a deep interest in the welfare of the younger men; for otherwise it might be objected, with perfect truth, that, if decisive power were placed in the hands of men of forty years of age, they would have an interest, just as any other detached portion of the community, in pursuing that career which we have already described, for reducing the rest of the community to the state of abject slaves. But the great majority of old men have sons, whose interest they regard as an essential part of their own. This is a law of human nature. There is, therefore, no great danger that, in such an arrangement as this, the interests of the young would be greatly sacrificed to those of the old.

We come next to the inquiry, whether the interest of a body of electors, constituted by the possession of a certain amount of property or income, would be the same with the interest of the community?

It will not be disputed, that, if the qualification were raised so high that only a few hundreds possessed it, the case would be exactly the same with that of the consignment of the Electoral Suffrage to an Aristocracy. This we have already considered, and have seen that it differs in form rather than substance from a simple Aristocracy. We have likewise seen, that it alters not the case in regard to the community, whether the Aristocracy be some hundreds or many thousands. One thing is, therefore, completely ascertained, that a pecuniary qualification, unless it were very low, would only create an Aristocratical Government, and produce all the evils which we have shown to belong to that organ of misrule.

This question, however, deserves to be a little more minutely considered. Let us next take the opposite extreme. Let us suppose that the qualification is very low, so low as to include the great majority of the people. It would not be easy for the people who have very little property, to separate their interests from those of the people who have none. It is not the interest of those who have little property to give undue advantages to the possession of property, which those who have the great portions of it would turn against themselves.

It may, therefore, be said, that there would be no evil in a low qualification. It can hardly be said, however, on the other hand, that there would be any good; for if the whole mass of the people who have some property would make a good choice, it will hardly be pretended that, added to them, the comparatively small number of those who have none, and whose minds are naturally and almost necessarily governed by the minds of those who have, would be able to make the choice a bad one.

We have ascertained, therefore, two points. We have ascertained that a very low qualification is of no use, as affording no security for a good choice beyond that which would exist if no pecuniary qualification was required. We have likewise ascertained, that a qualification so high as to constitute an Aristocracy of wealth, though it were a very numerous one, would leave the community without protection, and exposed to all the evils of unbridled power. The only question, therefore, is, whether, between these extremes, there is any qualification which would remove the right of Suffrage from the people of small, or of no property, and yet constitute an elective body, the interest of which would be identical with that of the community?

It is not easy to find any satisfactory principle to guide us in our researches, and to tell us where we should fix. The qualification must either be such as to embrace the majority of the population, or some thing less than the majority. Suppose, in the first place, that it embraces the majority, the question is, whether the majority would have an interest in oppressing those who, upon this supposition, would be deprived of political power? If we reduce the calculation to its elements, we shall see that the interest which they would have, of this deplorable kind, though it would be something, would not be very great. Each man of the majority, if the majority were constituted the governing body, would have something less than the benefit of oppressing a single man. If the majority were twice as great as the minority, each man of the majority would only have one-half the benefit of oppressing a single man. In that case, the benefits of good Government, accruing to all, might be expected to overbalance to the several members of such an elective body the benefits of misrule peculiar to themselves. Good Government, would, therefore, have a tolerable security. Suppose, in the second place, that the qualification did not admit a body of electors so large as the majority, in that case, taking again the calculation in its elements, we shall see that each man would have a benefit equal to that derived from the oppression of more than one man; and that, in proportion as the elective body constituted a smaller and smaller minority, the benefit of misrule to the elective body would be increased, and bad Government would be insured.

It seems hardly necessary to carry the analysis of the pecuniary qualification, as the principle for choosing an elective body, any farther.

We have only remaining the third plan for constituting an elective body. According to the scheme in question, the best elective body is that which consists of certain classes, professions, or fraternities. The notion is, that when these fraternities or bodies are represented, the community itself is represented. The way in which, according to the patrons of this theory, the effect is brought about, is this. Though it is perfectly true, that each of these fraternities would profit by misrule, and have the strongest interest in promoting it; yet, if three or four such fraternities are appointed to act in conjunction, they will not profit by misrule, and will have an interest in nothing but good Government.

This theory of Representation we shall not attempt to trace farther back than the year 1793. In the debate on the motion of Mr. (now Earl) Grey, for a Reform in the System of Representation, on the 6th of May, of that year, Mr. Jenkinson, the present Earl of Liverpool, brought forward this theory of Representation, and urged it in opposition to all idea of Reform in the British House of Commons, in terms as clear and distinct as those in which it has recently been clothed oy leading men on both sides of that House. We shall transcribe the passage from the speech of Mr. Jenkinson, omitting, for the sake of abbreviation, all those expressions which are unnecessary for conveying a knowledge of the plan, and of the reasons upon which it was founded.

" Supposing it agreed," he said, " that the House of Commons is meant to be a legislative body, representing all descriptions of men in the country, he supposed every person would agree, that the landed interest ought to have the preponderant weight. The landed interest was, in fact, the *stamina* of the country. In the second place, in a commercial country like this, the manufacturing and commercial interest ought to have a considerable weight, secondary to the landed interest, but secondary to the landed interest only. But was this all that was necessary? There were other descriptions of people, which, to distinguish them from those already mentioned, he should style professional people, and whom he considered as absolutely necessary to the composition of a House of Commons. By professional people, he meant those Members of the House of Commons who wished to raise themselves to the great offices of the State; those that were in the army, those that were in the navy, those that were in the law." He then, as a reason for desiring to have those whom he calls " professional people" in the composition of the House of Commons, gives it as a fact, that country Gentlemen and Merchants seldom desire, and seldom have motives for desiring, to be Ministers and other great Officers of State. These Ministers and Officers, however, ought to be made out of the House of Commons. Therefore, you ought to have " professional people" of whom to make them. Nor was this all. " There was another reason why these persons were absolutely necessary. We were constantly in the habit of discussing in that House all the important concerns of the State. It was necessary, therefore, that there should be persons in the practice of debating such questions." " There was a third reason, which, to his mind, was stronger than all the rest. Suppose that in that House there were only country Gentlemen, they would not then be the Representatives of the nation, but of the landholders. Suppose there were in that House only commercial persons, they would not be the Representatives of the nation, but of the commercial interest of the nation. Suppose the landed and commercial interest could both find their way into the House. The landed interest would be able, if it had nothing but the commercial interest to combat with, to prevent that interest from having its due weight in the Constitution. All descriptions of persons in the country would thus, in fact, be at the mercy of the landholders." He adds, " the professional persons are, then, what makes this House the Representatives of the people. They have collectively no *esprit de corps*, and prevent any *esprit de corps* from affecting the proceedings of the House. Neither the landed nor commercial interest can materially affect each other, and the interests of the different professions of the country are fairly considered. The Honourable Gentleman (Mr. Grey), and the petition on this table, rather proposed uniformity of election. His ideas were the reverse—

that the modes of election ought to be as varied as possible, because, if there was but one mode of election, there would, generally speaking, be but one description of persons in that House, and by a varied mode of election only could that variety be secured."

There is great vagueness undoubtedly in the language here employed; and abundant wavering and uncertainty in the ideas. But the ideas regarding this theory, appear in the same half-formed state in every speech and writing in which we have seen it adduced. The mist, indeed, by which it has been kept surrounded, alone creates the difficulty; because it cannot be known precisely how any thing is good or bad, till it is precisely known what it is.

According to the ideas of Lord Liverpool, the landholders ought to be represented; the merchants and manufacturers ought to be represented; the officers of the army and navy ought to be represented; and the practitioners of the law ought to be represented. Other patrons of the scheme have added, that literary men ought to be represented. And these, we believe, are almost all the fraternities which have been named for this purpose by any of the advocates of representation by clubs. To insure the choice of Representatives of the landholders, landholders must be the choosers; to insure the choice of Representatives of the merchants and manufacturers, merchants and manufacturers must be the choosers; and so with respect to the other fraternities, whether few or many. Thus it must be at least in *substance;* whatever the *form,* under which the visible acts may be performed. According to the scheme in question, these several fraternities are represented *directly,* the rest of the community is *not* represented directly; but it will be said by the patrons of that scheme, that it is represented *virtually,* which, in this case, answers the same purpose.

From what has already been ascertained, it will appear certain, that each of these fraternities has its sinister interest, and will be led to seek the benefit of misrule, if it is able to obtain it. This is frankly and distinctly avowed by Lord Liverpool. And by those by whom it is not avowed, it seems impossible to suppose that it should be disputed.

Let us now, then, observe the very principle upon which this theory must be supported. Three, or four, or five, or more clubs of men, have unlimited power over the whole community put into their hands. These clubs have, each, and all of them, an interest, an interest the same with that which governs all other rulers, in misgovernment, in converting the persons and properties of the rest of the community wholly to their own benefit. Having this interest, says the theory, they will not make use of it, but will use all their powers for the benefit of the community. Unless this proposition can be supported, the theory is one of the shallowest by which the pretenders to political wisdom have ever exposed themselves.

Let us resume the proposition. Three, or four, or five fraternities of men, composing a small part of the community, have all the powers of government placed in their hands. If they oppose and contend with one another, they will be unable to convert these powers to their own benefit. If they agree they will be able to convert them wholly to their own benefit, and to do with the rest of the community just what they please.

The patrons of this system of Representation assume, that these fraternities will be sure to take that course which is *contrary* to their interest. The course which is *according* to their interest, appears as if it had never presented itself to their imaginations!

There being two courses which the clubs may pursue, one contrary to their interest, the other agreeable to it, the patrons of the club system must prove, they must place it beyond all doubt, that the clubs will follow the first course, and not follow the second: if not, the world will laugh at a theory which is founded upon a direct contradiction of one of the fundamental principles of human nature.

In supposing that clubs or societies of men are governed, like men individually, by their interests, we are surely following a pretty complete experience. In the idea that a certain number of those clubs can unite to pursue a common interest, there is surely nothing more extraordinary, than that as many individals should unite to pursue a common interest. Lord Liverpool talks of an *esprit de corps* belonging to a class of landholders, made up of the different bodies of landholders in every county in the kingdom. He talks of an *esprit de corps* in a class of merchants and manufacturers, made up of the different bodies of merchants and manufacturers in the several great towns and manufacturing districts in the kingdom. What, then, is meant by an *esprit de corps*? Nothing else but a union for the pursuit of a common interest. To the several clubs supposed in the present theory, a common interest is created by the very circumstance of their composing the representing and represented bodies. Unless the patrons of this theory can prove to us, contrary to all experience, that a common interest cannot create an *esprit de corps* in men in combinations, as well as in men individually, we are under the necessity of believing, that an *esprit de corps* would be formed in the classes separated from the rest of the community for the purposes of Representation; that they would pursue their common interest; and inflict all the evils upon the rest of the community to which the pursuit of that interest would lead.

It is not included in the idea of this union for the pursuit of a common interest, that the clubs or sets of persons appropriated to the business of Representation should totally harmonize. There would, no doubt, be a great mixture of agreement and disagreement among them. But there would, if experience is any guide, or if the general laws of human nature have any power, be sufficient agreement to prevent their losing sight of the common interest; in other words, for insuring all that abuse of power which is useful to the parties by whom it is exercised.

The real effect of this motley Representation, therefore, would only be to create a motley Aristocracy; and, of course, to insure that kind of misgovernment which it is the nature of Aristocracy to produce, and to produce equally, whether it is a uniform, or a variegated Aristocracy; whether an Aristocracy all of landowners; or an Aristocracy in part landowners, in part merchants and manufacturers, in part officers of the army and navy, and in part lawyers.

We have now, therefore, examined the principles of the Representative system, and have found in it all that is necessary to constitute a security for good government: We have seen in what manner it is possible to prevent in the Representatives the rise of an interest different from that of the parties who choose them, namely, by giving them little time, not dependent upon the will of those parties: We have likewise seen in what manner identity of interest may be insured between the electoral body and the rest of the community: We have, therefore, discovered the means by which identity of interest may be insured between the Representatives and the community at large. We have, by consequence, obtained an organ of Government which possesses that quality, without which there can be no good Government.

IX.

1. *Objection: That a perfect Representative System, if established, would destroy the Monarchy, and the House of Lords.*

The question remains, Whether this organ is competent to the performance of the whole of the business of Government? And it may be certainly answered, that it is not. It may be competent to the making of laws, and it may watch over their execution: but to the executive functions themselves, operations in detail, to be performed by individuals, it is manifestly not competent. The executive functions of Government consist of two parts, the administrative and the judicial. The administrative, in this country, belong to the King; and it will appear indubitable, that, if the best mode of disposing of the administrative powers of Government be to place them in the hands of one great functionary, not elective, but hereditary; a King, such as ours, instead of being inconsistent with the Representative system, in its highest state of perfection, would be an indispensable branch of a good Government; and, even if it did not previously exist, would be established by a Representative body whose interests were identified, as above, with those of the nation.

The same reasoning will apply exactly to our House of Lords. Suppose it true, that, for the perfect performance of the business of Legislation, and of watching over the execution of the laws, a second deliberative Assembly is necessary; and that an Assembly, such as the British House of Lords, composed of the proprietors of the greatest landed estates, with dignities and privileges, is the best adapted to the end: it follows, that a body of Representatives, whose interests were identified with those of the nation, would establish such an Assembly, if it did not previously exist: for the best of all possible reasons; that they would have motives for, and none at all against it.

Those parties, therefore, who reason against any measures necessary for identifying the interests of the Representative body with those of the nation, under the plea that such a Representative body would abolish the King and the House of Lords, are wholly inconsistent with themselves. They maintain that a King and a House of Lords, such as ours, are important and necessary branches of a good Government. It is demonstratively certain that a Representative body, the interests of which were identified with those of the nation, would have no motive to abolish them, if they were not causes of bad government. Those persons, therefore, who affirm that it would certainly abolish them, affirm implicitly that they are causes of bad, and not necessary to good government. This oversight of theirs is truly surprising.

The whole of this chain of deduction is dependent, as we stated at the beginning, upon the principle that the acts of men will be conformable to their interests. Upon this principle, we conceive that the chain is complete and irrefragable. The principle, also, appears to stand upon a strong foundation. It is indisputable that the acts of men follow their will; that their will follows their desires; and that their desires are generated by their apprehensions of good or evil; in other words, by their interests.

X.

II. *Objection: That the People are not capable of acting agreeably to their Interest.*

The apprehensions of the people, respecting good and evil, may be just, or they may be erroneous. If just, their actions will be agreeable to their real interests. If erroneous, they will not be agreeable to their real interests, but to a false supposition of interest.

We have seen, that, unless the Representative Body are chosen by a portion of the community the interest of which cannot be made to differ from that of the community, the interest of the community will infallibly be sacrificed to the interest of the rulers.

The whole of that party of reasoners who support Aristocratical power affirm, that a portion of the community, the interest of whom cannot be made to differ from that of the community, will not act according to their interest, but contrary to their interest. All their pleas are grounded upon this assumption. Because, if a portion of the community whose interest is the same with that of the community, would act agreeably to their own interest, they would act agreeably to the interest of the community, and the end of Government would be obtained.

If this assumption of theirs is true, the prospect of mankind is deplorable. To the evils of misgovernment they are subject by inexorable destiny. If the powers of Government are placed in the hands of persons whose interests are not identified with those of the community, the interests of the community are wholly sacrificed to those of the rulers. If so much as a checking power is held by the community, or by any part of the community, where the interests are the same as those of the community, the holders of that checking power will not, according to the assumption in question, make use of it in a way agreeable, but in a way contrary to their own interest. According to this theory, the choice is placed between the evils which will be produced by design, the design of those who have the power of oppressing the rest of the community, and an interest in doing it; and the evils which may be produced by mistake, the mistake of those who, if they acted agreeably to their own interest, would act well.

Supposing that this theory were true, it would still be a question, between these two sets of evils, whether the evils arising from the design of those who have motives to employ the powers of Government for the purpose of reducing the community to the state of abject slaves of their will, or the evils arising from the misconduct of those who never produce evil but when they mistake their own interest, are the greatest evils.

Upon the most general and summary view of this question, it appears that the proper answer cannot be doubtful. They who have a fixed, invariable interest in acting ill, will act ill invariably. They who act ill from mistake, will often act well, sometimes even by accident, and in every case in which they are enabled to understand their interest, by design.

There is another, and a still more important ground of preference. The evils which are the produce of interest and power united, the evils on the one side, are altogether incurable: the effects are certain while that conjunction which is the cause of them remains. The evils which arise from mistake are not incurable; for, if the parties who act contrary to their interest had a proper knowledge of that interest, they would act well. What is necessary, then, is knowledge. Knowledge, on the part of those whose interests are the same as those of the community, would be an adequate remedy. But knowledge is a thing which is capable of being increased: and the more it is increased the more the evils on this side of the case would be reduced.

Supposing, then, the theory of will opposed to interest to be correct, the practical conclusion would be, as there is something of a remedy to the evils arising from this source, none whatever to the evils arising from the conjunction of power and sinister interest, to adopt the side which has the remedy, and to do whatever is necessary for obtaining the remedy in its greatest possible strength, and for applying it with the greatest possible efficacy.

It is no longer deniable that a high degree of knowledge is capable of being conveyed to such a portion of the community, as would have interests the same with those of the community. This being the only resource for good government, those who say that it is not yet attained stand in this dilemma; either they do not desire good government, which is the case with all those who derive advantage from bad; or they will be seen employing their utmost exertions to increase the quantity of knowledge in the body of the community.

The practical conclusion, then, is actually the same, whether we embrace or reject the assumption that the community are little capable of acting according to their own interest.

That assumption, however, deserves to be considered. And it would need a more minute consideration than the space to which we are confined will enable us to bestow upon it.

One caution, first of all, we should take along with us; and it is this, That all those persons who hold the powers of Government, without having an identity of interests with the community, and all those persons who share in the profits which are made by the abuse of those powers, and all those persons whom the example and representations of the two first classes influence, will be sure to represent the community, or a part having an identity of interest with the community, as incapable in the highest degree, of acting according to their own interest; it being clear that they who have not an identity of interest with the community, ought to hold the power of Government no longer, if those who have that identity of interest could be expected to act in any tolerable conformity with their interest. All representations from that quarter, therefore, of their incapability so to act, are to be received with suspicion. They come from interested parties, they come from parties who have the strongest possible interest to deceive themselves, and to endeavour to deceive others.

It is impossible that the interested endeavours of all those parties should not propagate, and for a long time successfully uphold, such an opinion, to whatever degree it might be found, upon accurate inquiry, to be without foundation.

A parallel case may be given. It was the interest of the priesthood, when the people of Europe were all of one religion, that the laity should take their opinions exclusively from them; because, in that case, the laity might be rendered subservient to the will of the Clergy, to any possible extent; and as all opinions were to be derived professedly from the Bible, they withdrew from the laity the privilege of reading it. When the opinions which produced the Reformation, and all the blessings which may be traced to it, began to ferment, the privilege of the Bible was demanded. The demand was resisted by the Clergy, upon the very same assumption which we have now under contemplation. " The people did not understand their own interest. They would be sure to make a bad use of the Bible. They would derive from it not right opinions, but all sorts of wrong opinions."*

There can be no doubt that the assumption, in the religious case, was borne out by still stronger appearance of evidence, than it is in the political. The majority of the people may be supposed less capable of deriving correct opinions from the Bible, than of judging who is the best man to act as a Representative.

Experience has fully displayed the nature of the assumption in regard to religion. The power bestowed upon the people, of judging for themselves, has been productive of good effects, to a degree which has totally altered the condition of human nature, and exalted man to what may be called a different stage of existence.

For what reason then, is it, we are called upon to believe, that, if a portion of the community, having an identity of interests with the whole community, have the power of choosing Representatives, they will act wholly contrary to their interests, and make a bad choice?

Experience, it will be said, establishes this conclusion. We see that

---

* A most instructive display of these and similar artifices for the preservation of mischievous power, after the spirit of the times is felt to be hostile to it, may be seen in Father Paul's *History of the Council of Trent*.

the people do not act according to their interests, but very often in opposition to them.

The question is between a portion of the community, which, if entrusted with power, would have an interest in making a bad use of it, and a portion which, though entrusted with power, would not have an interest in making a bad use of it. The former are any small number whatsoever; who, by the circumstance of being entrusted with power, are constituted an Aristocracy.

From the frequency, however great, with which those who compose the mass of the community act in opposition to their interests, no conclusion can, in this case, be drawn, without a comparison of the frequency with which those, who are placed in contrast with them, act in opposition to theirs. Now, it may with great confidence be affirmed, that as great a proportion of those who compose the Aristocratical body of any country, as of those who compose the rest of the community, are distinguished for a conduct unfavourable to their interests. Prudence is a more general characteristic of the people who are without the advantages of fortune, than of the people who have been thoroughly subject to their corruptive operation. It may surely be said, that if the powers of Government must be entrusted to persons incapable of good conduct, they were better entrusted to incapables who have an interest in good government, than to incapables who have an interest in bad.

It will be said that a conclusion ought not to be drawn from the unthinking conduct of the great majority of an Aristocratical body, against the capability of such a body for acting wisely in the management of public affairs; because the body will always contain a certain proportion of wise men, and the rest will be governed by them. Nothing but this can be said with pertinency. And, under certain modifications, this may be said with truth. The wise and good in any class of men do, to all general purposes, govern the rest. The comparison, however, must go on. Of that body, whose interests are identified with those of the community, it may also be said, that if one portion of them are unthinking, there is another portion wise; and that, in matters of state, the less wise would be governed by the more wise, not less certainly than in that body, whose interests, if they were entrusted with power, could not be identified with those of the community.

If we compare in each of these two contrasted bodies the two descriptions of persons, we shall not find that the foolish part of the Democratical body are more foolish than that of the Aristocratical, nor the wise part less wise.

Though, according to the opinions which fashion has propagated, it may appear a little paradoxical, we shall probably find the very reverse.

That there is not only as great a proportion of wise men in that part of the community which is not the Aristocracy, as in that which is; but that, under the present state of education, and the diffusion of knowledge, there is a much greater, we presume, there are few persons who will be disposed to dispute. It is to be observed, that the class which is universally described as both the most wise and the most virtuous part of the community, the middle rank, are wholly included in that part of the community which is not the Aristocratical. It is also not disputed, that in Great Britain the middle rank are numerous, and form a large proportion of the whole body of the people. Another proposition may be stated, with a perfect confidence of the concurrence of all those men who have attentively considered the formation of opinions in the great body of society, or, indeed, the principles of human nature in general. It is, that the opinions of that class of the people, who are below the middle rank, are formed, and their minds are directed by that intelligent and virtuous rank, who come the most immediately in contact with them, who are in the constant habit of intimate communication with them, to whom they fly for advice and assistance in all their numerous difficulties, upon whom they feel an immediate and daily dependence, in health and in sickness, in infancy and in old age; to whom their children look up as models for their imitation, whose opinions they hear daily repeated, and account it their honour to adopt. There can be no doubt that the middle rank, which gives to science, to art, and to legislation itself, their most distinguished ornaments, the chief source of all that has exalted and refined human nature, is that portion of the community of which, if the basis of Representation were ever so far extended, the opinion would ultimately decide. Of the people beneath them, a vast majority would be sure to be guided by their advice and example.

The incidents which have been urged as exceptions to this general rule, and even as reasons for rejecting it, may be considered as contributing to its proof. What signify the irregularities of a mob, more than half composed, in the greater number of instances, of boys and women, and disturbing, for a few hours or days, a particular town? What signifies the occasional turbulence of a manufacturing district, peculiarly unhappy from a very great deficiency of a middle rank, as there the population almost wholly consists of rich manufacturers and poor workmen; with whose minds no pains are taken by anybody; with whose afflictions there is no virtuous family of the middle rank to sympathize; whose children have no good example of such a family to see and to admire; and who are placed in the highly unfavourable situation of fluctuating between very high wages in one year, and very low wages in another? It is altogether futile with regard to the foundation of good government to say that this or the other portion of the people, may at this, or the other time, depart from the wisdom of the middle rank. It is enough that the great majority of the people never cease to be guided by that rank; and we may, with some confidence, challenge the adversaries of the people to produce a single instance to the contrary in the history of the world.

(F. F.)

THE ARTICLE

JURISPRUDENCE,

REPRINTED FROM

THE SUPPLEMENT

TO THE

ENCYCLOPÆDIA BRITANNICA.

JURISPRUDENCE.

I.

The end of Jurisprudence, viz. the Protection of Rights.—Importance of the Inquiry, as involving Human Happiness.—Confusion in the vulgar uses of the word Right.—Use of the term Right, in the Science of Jurisprudence.—The principal ideas involved in the Jurisprudential sense of the word Right.—All Rights respect Objects desired; and desired as means to an end.—The Objects of Rights are twofold, viz. either Persons or Things.—Rights, when closely inspected, mean Powers—*legalized* Powers.—Powers *over* Persons, *and* Powers *over* Things.—*Every Right imports a corresponding Obligation.—No Creation of Good, by Rights, without the Creation of Evil.*

THE object and end of the science which is distinguished by the name of Jurisprudence, is the protection of rights.

The business of the present discourse is, therefore, to ascertain the means which are best calculated for the attainment of that end.

What we desire to accomplish is, The protection of rights: What we have to inquire is, The means by which protection may be afforded.

That rights have hitherto been very ill protected, even in the most enlightened countries, is matter of universal acknowledgment and complaint. That men are susceptible of happiness, only in proportion as rights are protected, is a proposition, which, taken generally, it is unnecessary to prove. The importance of the inquiry, therefore, is evident.

It is requisite, as a preliminary, to fix, with some precision, what we denote by the expression *rights*. There is much confusion in the use of this term. That disorderly mass, the Roman law, changes the meaning of the word in stating its division of the subject, Jura Personarum, and Jura Rerum. In the first of these phrases, the word Jura means a title to enjoy; in the second, it must of necessity mean something else, because things cannot enjoy. Lawyers, whose nature it is to trudge, one after another, in the track which has been made or them; and to whose eyes, that which is, and that which ought to be, have seldom any mark of distinction, have translated the jargon into English, as well as into other modern languages.

This is not all the confusion which has been incurred in the use of the word *right*. It is sometimes employed in a very general way, to denote whatever ought to be; and in that sense is opposed to wrong. There are also persons—but these are philosophers, pushing on their abstractions—who go beyond the sense in which it is made to denote generally whatever ought to be, and who make it stand for the *foundation* of whatever ought to be. These philosophers say, that there is a right and a wrong, original, fundamental; and that things ought to be, or ought not to be, according as they do, or do not, conform to that standard. If asked, whence we derive a knowledge of this right and wrong in the abstract, which is the foundation and standard of what we call right and wrong in the concrete, they speak dogmatically, and convey no clear ideas.* In short, writers of this stamp give us to understand, that we must take this standard, like many other things which they have occasion for, upon their word. After all their explanations are given, this, we find, is what alone we are required, or rather commanded, to trust to. The standard exists,—Why? Because they say it exists; and it is at our peril if we refuse to admit the assertion. They assume a right, like other despots, to inflict punishment, for contumacy, or contempt of court. To be sure, hard words are the only instrument of tyranny which they have it in their power to employ. They employ them, accordingly; and there is scarcely an epithet, calculated to denote a vicious state of the intellectual, or moral part, of the human mind, which they do not employ to excite an unfavourable opinion of those who refuse subscription to their articles of faith.

With right, however, in this acceptation, we have at present, no farther concern than to distinguish it clearly from that sense in which the word is employed in the science of jurisprudence. To conceive more exactly the sense in which it is employed in that science, it is necessary to revert to what we established, in the article GOVERNMENT, with regard to the end or object of the social union, for to that, every thing which is done in subservience to the social union, must of course bear a reference.

In that article it appeared, that, as every man desires to have for himself as many good things as possible, and as there is not a sufficiency of good things for all, the strong, if left to themselves, would take from the weak every thing, or at least as much as they pleased; that the weak, therefore, who are the greater number, have an interest in conspiring to protect themselves against the strong. It also appeared, that almost all the things, which man denominates good, are the fruit of human labour; and that the natural motive to labour is the enjoyment of its fruits.

That the object, then, of the social union, may be obtained; in other

* See the writings of Kant and his followers, *passim*; see also Degerando, and others of his school, in various parts of their works.

words, that the weak may not be deprived of their share of good things, it is necessary to fix, by some determination, what shall belong to each, and to make choice of certain marks by which the share of each may be distinguished. This is the origin of right. It is created by this sort of determination, which determination is either the act of the whole society, or of some part of the society which possesses the power of determining for the whole. Right, therefore, is factitious, and the creature of will. It exists, only because the society, or those who wield the powers of the society, will that it should exist; and before it was so willed, it had no existence.

It is easy to see what is the standard, in conformity with which the rights in question *ought* to be constituted; meaning by *ought*, that which perfect benevolence would desire. It is the greatest happiness of the greatest number. But whether rights are constituted, that is, whether the shares of good things are allotted to each, according to this standard, or not according to this standard, the allotment is still the act of the ruling power of the community; and the rights, about which the science of jurisprudence treats, have this alone for the cause of their existence.

In this complicated term, it is obvious that there is involved, on the one hand, the idea of the person to whom a share is allotted, and on the other hand, an idea of the things which are allotted. The one is the owner of the right, the person to whom it belongs; the other is the object of the right, namely, the person or thing over which certain powers are given.

All rights of course are rights to objects of human desire,—of nothing else need shares be allotted. All objects which men desire, are desired, either as the end, or as means. The pleasurable state of the mind is the end; consisting of the feelings of the mind. It would be absurd, however, to speak of giving a man a right to the feelings of his own mind. The objects of desire, therefore, which are the objects of right, are not the pleasurable feelings themselves, which are desired as the end, but the objects which are desired as the means to that end.

Objects of desire, as means to that end, may be divided into the class of persons and the class of things. Both may be the object of rights. In framing our language, therefore, we may say, that all rights are the rights *of* persons; but they may be rights *to*, either persons, or things.

All that men desire, either with persons or things, is to render them subservient to the end, for which they are desired as means. They are so rendered by certain powers over them. All rights, then, when the term is closely investigated, are found to mean powers; powers with respect to persons, and powers with respect to things. What any one means when he says that a thing is his property, is, that he has the power of using it in a certain way.

It is no part of the present inquiry to ascertain what rights *ought* to be constituted, or what rights perfect benevolence would choose to see constituted That belongs to the question how government should be constituted; in other words, how the powers which are necessary for the general protection ought to be distributed, and the advantages of the union to be shared. At present our sole endeavour is to ascertain the most effectual means which the governing power of the state can employ for protecting the rights, whatever they are, which it has seen meet to create.

Rights, it must be remembered, always import obligations. This is a point of view, which, in the consideration of rights, has not, in general, attracted sufficient attention. If one man obtains a right to the services of another man, an obligation is, at the same time, laid upon this other to render those services. If a right is conferred upon one man to use and dispose of a horse, an obligation is laid upon other men to abstain from using him. It thus appears, that it is wholly impossible to create a right, without at the same time creating an obligation.

The consequences of this law of nature are in the highest degree important. Every right is a benefit; a command to a certain extent over the objects of desire. Every obligation is a burthen; an interdiction from the objects of desire. The one is in itself a good; the other is in itself an evil. It would be desirable to increase the good as much as possible. But, by increasing the good, it necessarily happens that we increase the evil. And, if there be a certain point at which the evil begins to increase faster than the good, beyond that point all creation of rights is hostile to human welfare.

The end in view is a command over the objects of desire. If no rights are established, there is a general scramble, and every man seizes what he can. A man gets so much, and he is interdicted by the scramble from all the rest. If rights are established, he also gets so much, and is interdicted by his obligations from the rest. If what he obtains by his rights exceeds what he would have obtained by the scramble, he is a gainer by the obligations which he sustains.

If it is proposed to create rights in favour of all the members of a community, the limits are strict. You cannot give all your advantages to every one; you must share them out. If you do not give equal rights to all, you can only give more than an equal share to some, by diminishing the share of others, of whom, while you diminish the rights, you increase the obligations. This is the course which bad governments pursue; they increase the rights of the few, and diminish the rights of the many, till, in the case of governments virtually despotic, it is all right on the one side, all obligation on the other.

It may be necessary to say a word, to prevent misconstruction of the term " equal rights." Rights may truly be considered as equal, if all the sorts of obligation under which a man lies with respect to other men, they are placed under with respect to him: if all the abstinence which he is obliged to practise with respect to their property, they are obliged to practise with respect to his; if all the rules by which he is bound not to interfere with their actions bind them equally not to interfere with his. It is evident, that inequality of fortune is not excluded by equality of rights. It is also evident, that, from equality of rights must always be excepted those who are entrusted with the powers of the community for the purposes of government. They have peculiar rights, and the rest of the community are under corresponding obligations. It is equally evident, that those must be excepted who are not *sui juris*, as children in non-age, who must be under the guidance of others. Of two such classes of persons the relation to one another, that is, their reciprocal rights and obligations, need to be regulated by particular rules.

It is presumed that these illustrations will suffice to fix, in the minds of our readers, the exact meaning which is intended, in the present discourse, to be attached to the word *rights*. The sequel is to be occupied in discovering the means which are most proper to be employed for affording *protection* to those rights.

II.

Meaning of the Word Protection, in the Jurisprudential Phrase, Protection of Rights.—The first Requisite to the Protection of Rights is to make them capable of being known.—Definition of Rights, the first Instrument of Protection.—Definition of the Acts by which Rights are violated, and the Application of Preventive Motives, another Instrument of Protection.—Civil and Penal Codes,—What. —Code of Procedure,—What.—Corpus Juris, or Body of Law,— What.

In the term protection, it is hardly necessary to give notice, that we do not here mean protection against foreign enemies; that protection which is to be yielded by employing armies against invaders. The protection, of which it is the business of jurisprudence to find out and to describe the means, is that which is required by one member of the community against the other members. The members of the community, each of whom endeavours to have as much as possible of the objects of desire, will be disposed to take those objects one from another; to take them, either by force, or by fraud. The means of preservation must, therefore, be found. Certain members of the community, as organs of government, are furnished with powers for that purpose. The question is, what powers are required; and in what manner are they to be employed?

In proceeding to present what may be called a sort of skeleton-map of the ill-explored country of Jurisprudence, it is necessary to warn the reader, that he must supply, by his own attention, what the limits of the work did not permit to be done for him. The several topics are rather indicated, than expounded. It is hoped they are indicated so clearly, that there will be no difficulty in spreading out the ideas in detail. It is necessary, however, that the reader should do this for himself. As the writer has not been able to dwell upon the several topics, though of the utmost importance, long enough to stamp the due impression of them upon the mind; unless the reader takes time to do this, by reflection on each topic, as it arrives, he will pass to the succeeding ones without due preparation, and the whole will be perused without interest, and without profit.

That a man's rights may be effectually secured, it is obviously necessary, in the first place, that they should be made capable of being accurately known. This seems to be so undeniable, that it would answer little purpose to enlarge in its illustration. It is, however, exceedingly necessary that the importance of this requisite should be clearly and adequately conceived. How can a man's rights be protected from encroachment, if what are his rights be uncertain or unknown? If the boundary by which his rights are distinguished is clear and conspicuous, it is in itself a protection. It warns off invaders; it serves to strike them with awe; for it directs the eyes and indignation of mankind immediately and certainly to the offender. Where the boundary, on the other hand, is obscure and uncertain, so far scope is allowed for encroachment and invasion. When the question, to which of two men an article of property belongs, comes for decision to the judge, it is easy, if accurate marks are affixed, to point out and determine the rights of each. If no marks are attached, or such only as are obscure and variable, the decision must be arbitrary and uncertain. To that extent the benefit derived from the creation and existence of rights is diminished.

It is, therefore, demonstrable, and we may say demonstrated (the demonstration not being difficult), that, in the inquiry respecting the means of protecting rights, the *Definition of Rights* may be entered at the head of the list. Without this, as the ground-work, all other means are ineffectual. In proportion as rights can be ascertained, are the judicial functions, and judicial apparatus, capable of being employed to any beneficial purpose: in proportion to the facility with which they can be ascertained, is the extent of the benefit which the judicial functions are enabled to secure.

Such, then, is the first of the means necessary for the protection of rights: That they may receive the most perfect possible protection, they must be as accurately as possible defined.

In supposing that rights have need of protection, we suppose that there are acts by which rights are violated. With regard to those acts, the object is twofold; to redress the evil of the act when it has taken place; and to prevent the performance of such acts in future. To prevent the performance, two classes of means present themselves; to watch till the act is about to be committed, and then to interpose; or, to create motives which shall prevent the will to commit. It is but a small number of cases in which the first can be done; the latter is, therefore, the grand desideratum. From the view of these circumstances we discover two other articles in the catalogue of means. Those acts by which rights are violated require to be made accurately known; in other words to be defined; and the motives which are fitted to prevent them must be duly applied. Motives sufficient to that end can only be found in the painful class; and the act by which they are applied is denominated punishment. The definition, therefore, of offences, or of the acts by which rights are violated and which it is expedient to punish; and the definition of the penalties by which they are prevented, are equally necessary with the definition of rights themselves. The reasons which demonstrate this necessity are so nearly the same with those which demonstrate the necessity of the definition of rights, that we deem it superfluous to repeat them.

The definition of rights constitutes that part of law which has been generally denominated the *Civil Code*. The definition of offences and punishments constitutes that other part of law which has been generally denominated the criminal or *Penal Code*.

When rights are distributed, and the acts by which they may be violated are forbidden, an agency is required, by which that distribution may be maintained, and the violators of it punished. That agency is denominated judicature. The powers, by which that agency is constituted, require to be accurately defined; and the mode in which the agency itself is to be carried on must be fixed and pointed out by clear and determinate rules. These rules and definitions prescribe the form and practice of the courts, or mode in which the judicial functions are performed; and constitute that branch of law which has been called the *Code of Procedure*.

These three codes, the civil code, the penal code, and code of procedure, form together the whole subject of jurisprudence. Of the three, it sufficiently appears, that the last exists only for the sake of the other two. Courts and their operations are provided that the provisions of the civil and penal codes may not be without their effect. It is to be considered, therefore, as subordinate, and merely instrumental, in respect to the other two. They form the main body of the law; this is an accessary to the main body, though an accessary of indispensable use. It would be of great advantage to affix characteristic names to distinguish from one another the main and accessary parts of law. Unexceptionable names, however, it is not easy to find. Mr. Bentham, the great improver of this branch of knowledge, has called the civil and penal codes together, by the name of "substantive law," the code of procedure by that of "adjective law;" not, we may be satisfied, because he approved of those names, but because the language hardly afforded others to which equal objections would not apply. In the very sense in which either the term accessary, or the term adjective can be applied to the code of procedure, both may be applied to the penal code, as it respects the civil. The penal code exists purely for the sake of the civil; that the rights, which are ordained by the legislature, and marked out by the terms of the code, may be saved from infringement. The civil code is therefore the end and object of all the rest. The code of procedure, however, is auxiliary to each of the other two; the penal code to no more than one.

Having now explained the nature of the three codes which constitute the body of law necessary for the protection of rights, it remains that we illustrate, as much in detail as our limits will permit, what is required for the perfection of each.

III.

What is required for the perfection of the Civil Code.—Operations preliminary to the Definition of Rights.—Two Things necessary for the Definition of a Right:—First, a Description of its Extent; Secondly, a Description of the Facts which give it a Beginning and an End.

The grand object of the civil code is the definition of rights. Rights are sometimes more, sometimes less extensive. Thus the right of a man to a horse, may solely extend to use him in riding from one stage to another; or it may extend to the power of doing with him as he pleases. In like manner, the rights of a man with respect to a person may extend only to some momentary service, or they may go the length of slavery. Even slavery itself does not imply rights always equally extensive. In some cases, it implies rights as extensive over the slave as over the inferior animals.

All rights, when the essence of them is spoken of, are powers; powers to an individual, which the governing members of the community guarantee; powers, more or less extensive, of making either a person or a thing subservient to the gratification of his desires. To be made to gratify the desire of an individual, is to be made to render him a *service*. And the term *service* may, fortunately, be applied to both persons and things. A man receives a service from the field when it produces a crop, as well as from the servant and the horse who ploughed it. In one meaning of the word service, it implies only active service, or that rendered by the voluntary operations of sentient beings. In the present case, however, it is employed to denote both active and passive services. It is evident, that in every case in which any thing inanimate is rendered subservient to the gratification of a desire, the service is, properly speaking, a passive service. It is also evident, that even animate beings are rendered subservient to the gratification of desires in a way which may equally be called passive.

It is necessary to request attention to the explanation which is here given of the meaning in which the term *service* is to be employed; as both the English and the Roman lawyers use it in a very restricted sense. Here it is employed to denote the whole of that ministration to the gratification of our desires, which we are entitled, in consequence of rights, to derive either from persons or from things. Rights are powers, and the powers are means for the obtaining of services. We have now, therefore, a language, by the help of which we may speak with tolerable clearness.

Our object is to define rights, and rights are powers. But these powers can be defined, only by a reference to the services which they are the means of obtaining.

The first thing, therefore, to be done for the definition of rights is, to make out a list of all the kinds of services, which the legislature permits an individual to derive, first, from persons, and secondly, from things. This would not be a matter of very great difficulty. It would be right to begin with the most simple cases, and go on to the more complex. Thus, of the services derivable from a person, some are limited to a single species of act, and that within a limited time, and at a particular place. Others are services, consisting of various acts, limited or not limited in space and time. And lastly, are the whole services which a man is capable of rendering ; without limitation as to either space or time. Considerable pains would be necessary to make the list complete ; and not only considerable pains, but considerable logic would be necessary, to classify the services, in other words, make them up into lots, the most convenient for the purpose in question; and to fix the extent of each by an exact definition. It is obvious, that as soon as all the possible gradations, in the services which one human being can render to another, are exhibited by such enumeration and assortment, it is easy for the legislature to point out exactly whatever portion of these services it is its will to give any individual a right to.

The same considerations apply to the class of things. In being made subservient to the gratification of our desires, they also render services. In proportion as a man has the right to derive those services from them, they are said to be his property. The whole of the services, which are capable of being derived from them, may, without much difficulty, be enumerated and classified ; and when they are so, those which it may be the pleasure of the legislature to make any one's property, may be very easily and distinctly pointed out.

We may take land for an example. All the different services which are capable of being derived from the land may be enumerated, and, being classed under convenient heads, may be referred to with perfect certainty; and any portion of them, which is made the property of any individual, may thus be accurately described. A man may have a right simply to pasture a field; to pasture it for a day, or a year, or a hundred years. He may have a right to crop it ; and that either in a particular manner, or in any manner he pleases; for a year, or for any other time. He may have a right to use it for any purpose, and that during a limited time, or an unlimited time. The services which it is capable of rendering may belong to him in common with a number of other persons, or they may all belong to himself.

In illustration of this subject we may notice a classification of the services derivable from the land, made, though very rudely, by the English law. Blackstone, who, like other English lawyers, has, on this, as on all other occasions, no idea of any other classification, than that which is made by the technical terms of the English law, has distinguished certain lots of the services derivable from the land, under the name of " Estates therein ; Estates with respect to, 1*st*, Quantity of interest; 2*dly*, Time of Enjoyment; 3*dly*, Number and connection of the tenants :" That is, estates in fee simple, comprehending the whole of the services which are capable of being derived from the land, unlimited in point of time; estates in fee tail, implying always limitation in point of time, and often a limitation in respect to some of the services; estates for years; estates at will; estates at sufferance; estates on condition; estates in remainder; estates in reversion; estates in jointenancy; estates in coparcenary; estates in common. The Roman law has made no enumeration or classification of the services derivable from any thing, not even from the land. It speaks of property in the abstract, and in two states; property in possession, and property in action. The English law does the same thing in regard to all other property but the land. " Property, in chattels personal, is either in possession or in action," says Blackstone. He does, indeed, add, " The property of chattels personal is liable to remainders, if created by will, to jointenancy, and to tenancy in common."

The services derivable from other articles of property than land, need not be divided under many heads. A piece of plate, for example, may render certain services without alteration of its form; it may be incapable of rendering other services till it has received an alteration of its form. It is chiefly, therefore, by limitation of time, that the various quantities of interest in such articles need to be determined. A man's right may extend to the use of a silver cup, for a day, or a year, or for his life. During this time the different services which it is capable of rendering have no occasion to be divided. They go naturally altogether. An unlimited right to its services implies the power of using it, either with or without alteration of its form, and without limitation of time. In most instances the limited right would be called loan, though, in the case of heirlooms and some others, there is a limited use to which the term loan is not customarily applied.

In speaking of the rights which a man may have to persons; as master, as father, as husband, and so on; there is one case so remarkable, that it requires a few words to be added in its explanation. It is that of one's own person. In this case the rights of the individual have no proper limitation beyond the obligations under which he is laid, in consequence either of the rights conferred upon others, or of the means which are thought necessary for protecting them.

If we have enabled our readers to form a tolerable conception of what we desire to be accomplished under the title of an enumeration and commodious classification of the services derivable from persons and things, we have performed what we proposed. The enumeration and classification, themselves, are evidently incommensurate with the design of an article in the present work. That they are practicable may be confidently taken for granted. In fact, they amount to nothing more than a description of the different degrees in which the property of a thing may be possessed; a point which is decided upon in every legal dispute. If this be done, from time to time, for one article after another, it may be done once for all.

We have already said, that rights are powers, powers for the obtaining of certain services. We have also said, that those powers can be defined only by a reference to the services which they are the means of obtaining. When those services are enumerated and classified, what remains is easy. A right to those services must begin; and it must end. The legislature has only to determine what fact shall be considered as giving a beginning to each right, and what shall be considered as putting an end to it, and then the whole business is accomplished.

It is evident that, for the definition of rights, two things are necessary. The first is, an exact description of the extent of the right; the second is, the description of the fact which gives birth to it. The extent of the right is described by reference to the lots of services, in the title to which services all rights consist. The facts, which the convenient enjoyment of rights has pointed out as the fittest for giving commencement to rights, have been pretty well ascertained from the earliest period of society; and there has, in fact, been a very great conformity with respect to them in the laws of all nations.

The following is an imperfect enumeration of them:—*An expression of the will of the legislature*, when it makes any disposition with regard to property; *Occupancy*, when a man takes what belongs to nobody; *Labour; Donation; Contract; Succession.* Of these six causes of the commencement of a right there is a remarkable distinction between the first three and the last three. The first three give commencement to a right in favour of one individual, without necessarily putting an end to a right enjoyed by any other individual. The last three give commencement to a right in favour of one individual, only by making the same right to cease in favour of another individual. When a man, by donation, gives a horse to another man, the horse ceases to be the property of the one man by the very same act by which he becomes the property of the other; so in the case of sale, or any other contract.

It is necessary for the legislature, in order that each man may know what are the objects of desire which he may enjoy, to fix, not only what are the facts which shall give commencement to a right, but what are the facts which shall put an end to it. In respect to these facts, also, there is a great harmony in the laws of all nations.

There is first the will of the legislature. When it confers a right, it may confer it, either for a limited, or for an unlimited time. In the term unlimited time, we include the power of tradition, or transfer, in all its shapes. If the time is limited, by the declaration of the legislature, either to a certain number of years, or the life of the party, the fact which terminates the right is obvious. If a man possesses a right, unlimited in point of time, the events are three by which it has been commonly fixed that it may be terminated; 1. some expression of his own will, in the way of gift or contract; 2. some act of delinquency; or 3. his death.

The possessor of a right, unlimited in point of time, may, in the way of gift or contract, transfer his right either for a limited or for an unlimited time. Thus the owner of a piece of land may lease it for a term of years. He may also, in this way, convey the whole of the services which it is capable of rendering, or only a part of them. In this transaction, one event gives birth to a right in favour of the man who receives the lease, and terminates a right which was possessed by the man who gives it; and another event, namely, the arrival of the period assigned for the termination of the lease, terminates the right of the man who had received the lease, and revives the former right of the man who gave it.

Acts of delinquency have been made to terminate rights, by the laws of most nations, in the various modes of forfeiture and pecuniary penalty.

The mode in which the event of death should terminate rights has been variously regulated. Sometimes it has been allowed to terminate them simply; and what a man left at his death was open to the first occupant. All but rude nations, however, have determined the persons to whom the rights which a man possessed without limitation of time shall pass at his death. The will of the former owner, when expressed, is commonly allowed to settle the matter. When that is not expressed, it has by most legislators been regulated, that his rights shall pass to his next of kin.

What is the extent of each right; by what event it shall receive its commencement; and by what event it shall be terminated;—this is all which is necessary to be pre-determined with respect to it. To do this is the duty of the legislature. When it is done, the inquiry of the judge is clear and simple. Does such a right belong to such a man? This question always resolves itself into two others. Did any of the events, which give commencement to a right, happen in this case? And did any of those events, which terminate a right, not happen in this case? These are questions of fact, as distinguished from law; and are to be determined by the production of evidence. If a man proves that an event which gives commencement to a right, happened in his case, and if another man cannot prove that an event which terminates a right happened subsequently in that case, the right of the first man is established.

If we have now ascertained the importance and practicability of a civil code, and have shown what is to be done in order to obtain the benefit of it, we shall conclude, with some confidence, that we have rendered a great service to mankind. We proceed to the consideration of the penal code. The object of that code is, the acts by which rights may be violated.

IV.

What is necessary to the Perfection of the Penal Code.—Acts meet for Punishment.—What is required to the Definition of an Offence.

In the term violation, we include all those acts by which the powers, conveyed by a right, are prevented from operating according to the will of the owner.

With respect to a part of such acts, all that it is found convenient to do, through the instrumentality of judicature, is, to remove the obstruction which prevents the enjoyment of the right, without inflicting any penalty for creating it. Thus, if a debt is not paid when due, the right is violated of the man who ought to receive it. Enough, however, is in this case supposed to be done, if the man who owes the debt is constrained to make payment. The act of secretly abstracting, with a view to appropriate, a property of perhaps less value, would be an act which the laws of all nations would punish as theft.

Of injurious acts, those alone, to the commission of which it has been deemed expedient that penalties should be annexed, are considered as the object of the penal code. Of injurious acts so perfect an analysis has been exhibited by Mr. Bentham; so perfectly, too, have the grounds been laid down upon which those acts which are destined for punishment should be selected from the rest; and so accurately have the principles, according to which punishment should be meted out, been established, by that great philosopher, that, on this part of the subject, the philosophy of law is not far from complete.

As acts are declared to be offences, and are made subject to punishment, solely for the protection of rights, it is evident, that all acts which enter into the penal code, are acts which infringe upon rights, either directly, or indirectly. Those which infringe upon rights *directly*, are those by which injury is done to some individual or individuals; a blow, for example, an act of theft, and so on. We include also, under this division, all acts the *effects* of which produce an immediate infringement of rights; destroying a mound, for example, to inundate the lands of another man; importation of infection, by which the health or lives of others may be destroyed. Those acts by means of which rights are affected *indirectly*, are those which bear immediately upon the means which the state has provided for the protection of rights. The means which the state has provided for the protection of rights, are the operations of government generally. All acts, therefore, meet for punishment, are acts which disturb either individuals in the enjoyment of their rights, or the operations required for the protection of those rights. The latter, though mediately, and not immediately hurtful, are apt to be more extensively mischievous than the former. An act which infringes upon a right immediately, is commonly injurious only to one individual, or a small number of individuals; an act which prevents any of the operations of government from proceeding in its natural course is injurious to all those individuals to whose protection the due course of that operation is useful. Permit acts which interrupt all the operations of government, and all rights are practically destroyed.

If, as it thus appears, acts are meet for punishment, only because they infringe upon a right, or because they interrupt the operations provided for the protection of rights, it is evident, that, in the definition of one set of those acts, must be included the specification of the right which is infringed; and, in the definition of the other, must be included the specification of the operation disturbed. Before, therefore, an accurate penal code can exist, there must exist an accurate civil code, and also what we may call a constitutional or political code; the latter consisting of an accurate definition of the powers created for the purposes of government, and of the limitations applied to their exercise.

From what has been said, it may appear, that the definition of offences by which name we shall hereafter distinguish punishable acts, consists necessarily of two parts. The first part is the specification of the right infringed, or the operation of government disturbed; and the second part is the definition of the mode. Thus, for the definition of an act of theft, the right which the act has violated must be distinctly marked, and also the mode in which the violation has been committed. In the same class of offences, those against property for example, the mode in which the violation is performed is that chiefly which constitutes the difference between one offence and another. In a theft and a robbery, the right violated may be exactly the same; the mode in which the violation was effected constitutes the difference.

For several purposes of the penal code, it is useful, that, in the specification of the right violated, the value of what has been violated, in other words, the amount of the evil sustained, should sometimes be included. It is evident, that the value of rights can be judged of ultimately, only by a reference to human feelings. Of these feelings, however, certain outward marks must be taken as the standard. In offences which concern property the modes of aluation are familiarly known. In injuries to the person, those marks which denote injuries regarded by mankind in general as differing in magnitude; the size, for example, or position, of a wound; in injuries to reputation, the words used, and the occasion when, and so forth, are the only means of distinction which can be employed.

It may be necessary also to remark, that, in that part of the definition which relates to the mode, are to be distinguished the parties, when more than one, who engage in the same offence with different degrees of criminality; meaning, by different degrees of criminality, nothing more than demand for different degrees of punishment. The chief classes of such persons are those of principals and accessaries; and of accessaries both those before and those after the fact.

In the definition of the mode, the act is first to be described in its ordinary shape. The act, however, may be attended with aggravating circumstances on the one hand, or extenuating circumstances on the other; presenting a demand for increased punishment in the first case, and diminished punishment in the second. Mr. Bentham has logically remarked, that the circumstances which are to be regarded as aggravating, and the circumstances which are to be regarded as extenuating, being pretty nearly the same in all cases, they may be defined, in a separate chapter, once for all. This being done, the code proceeds in the following manner:—The definition is given of the offence in its ordinary shape, and the appropriate punishment is annexed; then immediately follows the same offence with aggravating circumstances; punishment so much the more severe: the same offence with extenuating circumstances; punishment so much the less.

Thus far we have spoken of the definition of offences, into which we have entered the less in detail, because we do not think there is much of controversy on the subject. Many persons, who doubt the possibility of framing a civil code, though, after the preceding exposition of the subject, it is a doubt which could not, we should imagine, very easily maintain itself, allow, that offences may all be defined; and that it is possible to prevent the monstrous iniquity of punishing men for acts as offences which they have not the means of knowing to be such.

V.

The Doctrine of Punishment.—Satisfaction.—Penalties.

After offences comes the consideration of the punishment to be annexed to them. This is a subject of considerable detail; it has been, however, so fully and admirably treated by Mr. Bentham, that only some of the more general considerations, necessary to mark out the place and importance of the topic, need here to be introduced.

When a right has been infringed, there are two things, it is evident, which ought to be done: The injury which has been sustained by the individual ought to be repaired: And means ought to be taken to prevent the occurrence of a like evil in future.

The doctrine of Satisfaction is not at all difficult, as far as regards the regulating principles; the complication is all in the detail. The greater number of injuries are those which concern property. A pecuniary value can generally be set upon injuries of this sort; though it is not very easy to determine the *pretium affectionis*, a matter of considerable importance, which the English law, so much made up of clumsiness in one part, and false refinement in another, wholly overlooks. For injuries to the person, also, it is most frequently in the pecuniary shape alone that any compensation can be made. In making these estimates, some general marks are all that can be conveniently defined by the law, and a considerable discretion must be left to the judge. Indeed, the question of damages is always a question of fact, which must be determined by the evidence adduced in each instance.

It accords with the feelings of every man to say, that he who has committed an injury, should be made to repair it. One part of punishment, therefore, ought, wherever special reason does not forbid, to consist in making satisfaction to the party injured. Pecuniary satisfaction, where the delinquent is rich, may be a small part of the due punishment; still, however, there is an obvious propriety, in making it a part so far as it can go. In the cases in which the delinquent has no property, there is the same propriety in making his labour subservient to that end. Hard labour, with the most economical fare, till the produce of the labour equals the amount of the satisfaction required, is, therefore, a species of punishment, recommended by the strongest considerations. It is not said that labour so limited would always be sufficient punishment, and there are many cases in which it would be too much; but even then, it should go as far as it can in the one case, and as far as it ought in the other.

When the injury is done to reputation, there is a manifest propriety in making the injurer contribute to the reparation, wherever it can be done. In many of the cases, too, the proper mode is abundantly obvious: all those, for example, where the publication of falsehood is the injurious act. The author of the injury may, in a way as public as that of the offence, and as well calculated as possible for the reparation of the injury, be obliged to declare that he has been solemnly adjudged to have propagated a falsehood, and is condemned to publish his own shame.

In the case of those offences which affect rights indirectly, namely, by affecting the securities provided for them, satisfaction seldom can have any place, because not any determinate individual or individuals have sustained an injury.

This may suffice, in exposition of the first thing which is desirable where an injury has been committed, namely, that reparation should be made. The second is, that measures should be adopted for preventing the future occurrence of similar events.

Acts are performed, only because there are motives to the performance of them. Of course injurious acts are performed, only because there are motives to the performance of them.

Corporal restraint being out of the question where all the members of the community are concerned, it is evident that only two means remain for preventing injurious acts; either, first, to take away the motives which provoke to them; or, secondly, to apply motives sufficient for the prevention of them.

From the very nature of many of the acts it is impossible to take away the motives which provoke to them. From property stolen it is impossible to detach the value of the property; from vengeance it is impossible to detach the hope of that relief which is sought by the blow that is aimed.

What is wanted, then, is a sufficiency of motive in each instance to counteract the motives which lead to the crime. Whatever the motives of the alluring kind which lead to an act, if you give stronger motives of the same kind to abstain from the act, the act will, of course, be prevented. The man who would steal from you 5*l*. will assuredly not do so, if he knows that he shall receive 6*l*. for abstaining.

The question may then be started, Why should not all crimes be prevented in this way, since reward is much more desirable and humane than punishment? The answer is most satisfactory, and is built upon a ground which ought to receive profound attention, on many occasions, on which it is treated with the most perfect disregard. No reward can be given to one man, or set of men, but at the expence of some other man or set of men. What is reward to one is therefore punishment to others. If 6*l*. be given to the man who would steal 5*l*., it must be taken from some one or more individuals of the community. If one man is elevated by any title or distinction, all the rest with regard to him are degraded and depressed. This is utterly unavoidable. The one event is necessarily included in the other. The giving of rewards, therefore, is a matter of serious import. It is not that simple act, that pure creation of good, which it is often so fraudulently given out to be, and so credulously and foolishly admitted to be.

Other reasons, which prove the insufficiency of rewards for preventing injurious acts, are too obvious to require to be mentioned. We shall not therefore dwell upon this topic. This at least is sufficiently evident, that to counteract the motives which lead to the commission of an act, we have but two methods. If we cannot apply motives, of the pleasurable sort, to induce the party to abstain from committing the act, we must apply such motives, of the painful sort, as will outweigh the motives which prompt to the performance. To prevent, by such means, a theft of 5*l*.; it is absolutely necessary to affix to that act a degree of punishment which shall outweigh the advantage of possessing 5*l*.

We have now, it is evident, obtained the principle by which punishment ought to be regulated : We desire to prevent certain acts : That is our end, and the whole of our end : We shall assuredly prevent any acts, if we attach to them motives of the painful kind, sufficient to outweigh the motives of the opposite kind which lead to the performance. If we apply a less quantity of evil than is sufficient for outweighing those motives, the act will still be performed, and the evil will be inflicted to no purpose ; it will be so much suffering in waste. If we apply a greater quantity of evil than is necessary, we incur a similar inconvenience ; we create a quantity of evil which is absolutely useless ; the act, which it is the tendency of the motives of the pleasurable kind to produce, will be prevented, if the motives of the painful kind outweigh them in the smallest degree, as certainly as if it outweigh them to any degree whatsoever. As soon, therefore, as the legislator has reached that point, he ought immediately to stop. Every atom of punishment which goes beyond is so much uncompensated evil, so much human misery created without any corresponding good. It is pure unmingled mischief.

As no exact measure, indeed, can be taken of the quantity of pain which will outweigh a supposed quantity of pleasure, it is sometimes necessary to risk going somewhat beyond the mark, in order to make sure of not falling short of it. And, in the case of acts of which the evil is very great ; of the higher order of crimes, in short ; it may be expedient to risk a considerable degree of excess in order to make sure of reaching the point of efficiency.

In estimating the quantity of evil which it may be necessary to create, in order to compensate the motive which leads to a mischievous act, two circumstances should be taken into the account. These are, certainty and proximity. It is of the less importance here to enter far into the illustration of these topics, because they are now pretty generally understood. It is well known that the prospect of an evil which is to happen within an hour, or two hours, produces a much greater uneasiness, than the prospect of the very same evil removed to the distance of years. Every man knows that he will die within a certain number of years; many are aware that they cannot live beyond a few years; and this knowledge produces no uneasiness. The effort, on the other hand, which enables a man to behave with tranquillity, on the prospect of immediate death, is supposed to be so difficult, that it is this which makes the hero. It is, therefore, of the greatest importance, that punishment should be immediate; because, in that case, a much smaller quantity of evil suffices. It is imperatively required, by the laws of benevolence, that, if evil is a necessary means to our end, every expedient should be used to reduce it to the smallest quantity possible. It is cruelty; it belongs only to a malignant nature; to apply evil in a way which demands a quantity of it greater than would otherwise have been required. Suppose a law, that no act of theft should be punished or challenged till twenty years after the commission, or till the life of the thief was supposed to be near its end. It is evident that all punishment, in this case; that death, in the greatest torture, would be nearly destitute of power. This is partly the ground of the complaint, of the little efficacy of religious punishment, though dreadful beyond expression in the degree.

The want of certainty is a defect of equal importance. If it is a matter of doubt, whether a threatened evil will take place, the imagination is prone to magnify the chance of its not happening; and, by indulgence, magnifies it to such a degree, that the opposite chance at last excites a comparatively feeble influence. This is a remarkable law of human nature, from the influence of which even the most wise and prudent of men are not exempt; and of which the influence is predominant in those inconsiderate minds which are the most apt to give way to the allurements of vice. To illustrate this law, the influence of the religious punishments affords the most instructive of all examples. The punishments themselves go far beyond what the imagination can conceive. It is the complaint of divines, and the observation of all the world, that, with the great body of men, the efficacy of them is exceedingly small. The reason is, that to the want of proximity is added the greatest uncertainty. If a man puts his finger in the candle, he knows that he will be punished, and immediately, by being burned. If a man commits even a heinous sin, he has no fear of receiving the religious punishment immediately, and he conceives that, in the mercy of his Judge, in repentance and faith, he has a chance of escaping it altogether. This chance his imagination exaggerates, and most men can, in this way, go on sinning with tranquillity, to the end of their days. If all punishments were as certain and immediate as that of putting a finger in the candle, the smallest quantity, it is evident, beyond what would form a counterbalance to the advantage of the forbidden act, would suffice for its prevention. If uncertainty is admitted, to any considerable degree, no quantity of evil will suffice. It is a fact, which experience has most fully established, and which is now recognized in the most vulgar legislation, that undue severity of punishment runs counter to its end. This it does by increasing uncertainty; because men are indisposed to be the instruments of inflicting evil by which their feelings are lacerated. That legislation, therefore, is bad, which does not take measures for the greatest possible degree of proximity and certainty in the punishments which it applies.

The sources are three, from which motives of the painful sort, applicable to the purposes of the legislator, are capable of being drawn:—
1. The physical; 2dly, The moral; and, 3dly, The religious.

I. Pains from the Physical Source may be communicated to a man through,
1. His person,
2. His connections,
3. His property.

Through his person, they may be communicated in four principal ways,—by death, disablement, restraint and constraint, simple pain.

A man's connections are either public or private; private, as spouse, parent, servant, master, &c.; public, as ruler, subject, teacher, scholar, and so on.

The modes in which a man is punished through his property need no explanation.

II. Pains, from the Moral Source, are the pains which are derived from the unfavourable sentiments of mankind. For the strength of the pains, derived from this source, we must refer to the writers who have treated of this part of human nature. It is sufficient here to advert to what is universally recognized, that these pains are capable of rising to a height, with which hardly any other pains, incident to our nature, can be compared; that there is a certain degree of unfavourableness in the sentiments of his fellow creatures, under which, hardly any man, not below the standard of humanity, can endure to live.

The importance of this powerful agency for the prevention of injurious acts, is too obvious to need to be illustrated. If sufficiently at command, it would almost supersede the use of other means. It is, therefore, one of the first objects to the legislator to know, in what manner he can employ the pains of the popular sanction with the greatest possible effect.

To know how to direct the unfavourable sentiments of mankind, it is necessary to know in as complete, that is, in as comprehensive a way as possible, what it is which gives them birth. Without entering into the metaphysics of the question, it is a sufficient practical answer, for the present purpose, to say, that the unfavourable sentiments of men are excited by every thing which hurts them. They love that which gives them pleasure; hate that which gives them pain. Those acts of other men which give them pleasure or save them from pain, acts of beneficence, acts of veracity, and so on, they love. Acts, on the other hand, which give them pain, mendacity, and so on, they hate. These sentiments, when the state of mind is contemplated out of which the acts are supposed to arise, are transformed into approbation and disapprobation, in all their stages and degrees; up to that of the highest veneration, down to that of the deepest abhorrence and contempt.

The unfavourable sentiments, which the legislator would excite towards forbidden acts, must, therefore, in each man, arise from his conception of the mischievousness of those acts. That conception depends upon three circumstances; 1*st*, The view which he himself takes of the act; 2*dly*, The view which appears to be taken by other people; 3*dly*, Every thing which operates to render more or less permanently present to his mind his own and other men's conception of its mischievousness. From these circumstances, the practical rules for applying this great power, as an instrument of the legislator for the prevention of mischievous acts, are easily deduced. 1. Let the best measures be taken for giving the people a correct view of the mischievousness of the act; and then their unfavourable sentiments will be duly excited. 2. Let proper pains be taken that the people shall know every mischievous act that is committed, and know its author; that, so, no evil act may, by concealment, escape the punishment which their unfavourable sentiments imply. 3. Let the legislature, as the leading section of the public, make publication of its own unfavourable sentiments; let it brand the act with infamy. 4. Let the same publication of his own unfavourable sentiments be made by the judge in the shape of reprimand and other declarations. 5. The legislature may increase the effect of these declarations, where the case requires it, by symbolical marks; or, 6, by personal exposure. 7. The legislature may so order matters in certain cases, that the mischievous act can be done only through another act already infamous; as when it is more infamous to break a vow to God than to make false declarations to men, a witness may be made to swear that he will tell the truth. 8. As the favourable sentiments of mankind are so powerfully excited towards wealth, a man suffers through the popular sanction when his property is so diminished as to lessen his rank.

III. In pointing and proportioning the apprehension of divine punishment, the legislator can do three things:

1. He can declare his own apprehension, and the measure of it, which should be as exactly proportioned as possible to the mischievousness of the acts:

2*dly*, He can hire other people to declare similar apprehensions, and to make the most of the means which are available for their propagation:

3*dly*, He may discountenance the pointing of religious apprehensions to any acts which are not mischievous; or the pointing of them more strongly to acts which are slightly, than to acts which are deeply mischievous. Whatever power of restraining from mischievous acts may be lodged in religious apprehensions, is commonly misapplied and wasted. It would be worth the cost, therefore, of pretty forcible means to prevent such a misapplication and waste of religious fears.*

In drawing from one, or more, of all these sources, a lot of punishment adapted to each particular case, the following properties, desirable in a lot of punishment, ought to be steadily borne in view. Every lot of punishment ought, as much as possible, to be,

1. Susceptible of graduation, so as to be applied in different degrees.
2. Measurable, that the difference of degrees may be duly ascertained.
3. Equable, that is, calculated to operate with uniform intensity upon all persons.
4. Such, that the thought of the punishment may naturally excite the thought of the crime.
5. Such, that the conception of it may be naturally vivid and intense.
6. Public, addressed to the senses.
7. Reformative.
8. Disabling; viz. from crime.
9. Remediable; viz. if afterwards found to be undeserved.
10. Compensative; viz. to the party injured.
11. Productive; viz. to the community, as labour.

Of all the instruments of punishment which have yet occured to the ingenuity of man, there is none which unites these desirable qualities in any thing like an equal degree with the *Panopticon Penitentiary*, as devised and described by Mr. Bentham.

One general rule applies, in the case of all the lots of punishment. It is this: That the private good which has operated as the motive to the injurious action, should, in all possible cases, be cut off, and the expected enjoyment prevented. Where this can be done completely, all the additional punishment necessary is only that which would suffice to compensate the want of certainty and proximity in the act of deprivation; for no man would commit a crime which he was sure he could not profit by; no man would steal, if he knew that the property stolen would that minute be taken from him. The interests which are capable of being promoted by a criminal act, may be summed up under the following titles:

1. Money, or money's worth.

---

* Nothing which can in any degree interfere with the rights of conscience, including whatever interpretation any man may put upon the words of Scripture, is here understood. It is the object of the legislator to encourage acts which are useful, prevent acts which are hurtful, to society. But religious hopes and fears are often applied, not to promote acts which are useful, prevent acts which are hurtful, to society; in which way, alone, they are capable of conducing to the views of the legislator; but to mere ceremonies. And cases are not wanting in which they are applied to produce acts that are hurtful, prevent those that are useful, to society. As far as religious motives are attached to the useful, instead of the useless or hurtful objects, society is benefited. It is this benefit which it is recommended to the legislator to pursue.

2. Power.
3. Revenge.
4. Vanity, emulation.
5. Sensual pleasure, chiefly venereal.
6. Safety in respect to legal punishment.

With respect to four of these interests, viz. money, power, vanity, and safety in respect to legal punishment, the contemplated benefit is capable, in many cases, of being completely intercepted.

In the case in which revenge has operated through the degradation of the party suffering, the evil doer may be disappointed by re-exaltation of the degraded party.

Sensual pleasure, having been enjoyed, is beyond the reach of this operation.

It is highly worthy of observation, that, among the advantages constituting the motives to crime, those which can be cut off, and from the enjoyment of which the offender can be precluded, constitute by far the most frequent incentives to crime.

This must suffice as a summary of what should be said on the mode of applying pain most usefully for the prevention of certain acts. It only remains to add, that the following are the cases in which it may be pronounced unfit that pain should be employed for that purpose:

1. Where the evil to the community does not overbalance the good to the individual.
2. Where the evil necessary for the punishment would outweigh the evil of the act.
3. Where the evil created is not calculated to prevent the act.
4. Where the end could be obtained by other means.

VI.

The Code of Procedure.—First stage of the Judicial Business.—Second stage of the Judicial Business.

We have now, therefore, stated, what the limits of this discourse enable us to adduce, on the subject of the main body of the law; the enactments of the legislature with respect to rights, and with respect to those acts by which rights are violated. It remains that we consider that subsidiary branch of law, by which an agency is constituted for the purpose of carrying those enactments into effect. The inquiry here is, 1. what are the operations essential to that agency; 2. by what agents are they most likely to be well performed; and 3. what are the best securities that can be taken for the good conduct of these agents.

It most significantly illustrates the manner in which ignorance gropes its way in the dark, to observe, that the agency, the sole end of which is to carry into execution the civil and penal laws, was created first, and was in operation for ages, before the idea of the other branches of law was even tolerably framed. It is also worthy of remark, that the men, whose wisdom rules our affairs, are in the habit of calling the mode in which ignorance gropes its way in the dark, by the name of experience; the mode of acting upon a plan, and with foresight, by the names of theory and speculation.

There is instruction, in observing the mode, in which this inverted course of law-making was pursued. Men disputed; and their disputes were attended with the most destructive consequences. Originally, the king, at the head of the military force, and his subordinates, each at the head of a section of that force, interfered in those disputes. After a time, the king appointed functionaries, under the name of judges, for that particular service. These judges decided, without any rule, by their own discretion. The feelings of the community, grounded upon their experience of what tended to good and evil upon the whole, pointed vaguely to certain things as right, to other things as wrong; and to these the judge, as often as he was in *bona fides*, conformed his decision. The mode was similar both in arbitrating, and in punishing.

As punishing, especially in the severer cases, was an act which made a vivid impression upon the mind, the mode in which that act had been performed in previous cases was apt to be remembered: of the several modes, that which was most approved by the public would naturally be followed the most frequently; and at last there would be a species of scandal, if it was unnecessarily departed from. In this way a uniformity, more or less perfect, was established, in punishing the more heinous offences; and in regard to them custom first established what had some feeble portion of the attributes of a law.

In those cases in which, without a call for punishment, the authoritative termination of a dispute was all that was required, the experience of what was necessary, not only for any degree of mutual comfort, but even for the means of subsistence, soon established a few leading points of uniformity. Thus, when a man had cultivated a piece of ground, which belonged to nobody more peculiarly than to himself, it was evidently necessary that the crop should be considered as belonging to him; otherwise, no crops would be raised, and the community would be deprived of the means of subsistence.

These general feelings, with the remembrance, more or less perfect, of what had been done in similar cases, were the only guide; and it is surprising to what an extent, over the surface of the whole globe, law has, in all ages, remained in that state of imperfect existence, if, indeed, with any propriety, it can be called a state of existence. In every part of Asia, and in all ages, law has remained in that state of existence, or non-existence. In Europe, where, at a pretty early period, it became the practice to record in writing the proceedings of the judges, the natural propensity of referring to the past as a rule for the present, begat in time a species of obligation of being directed by the examples which had already been set. This created a uniformity and certainty, which, however imperfect, afforded something better than the arbitrary proceedings of Asiatic judges. Yet this was a benefit which had a dreadful alloy.

A body, not of law, but of decisions, out of which, on each particular occasion, a law for that particular occasion, as out of the crude ore, was to be smelted, hammered, and wire-drawn, was the natural material out of which to manufacture a system of chicane. How accurately the system of law, in the several nations of Europe, has conformed to the character of a system of chicane, is matter of present and lamentable experience. The uncertainty, the delay, the vexation and expence, and that immorality of the worst species with which they inundate the community, are not the only evils, great as they are, of laws constructed upon such a plan. A system of laws, so constructed, becomes an instrument of conversation for the barbarous customs and ideas of the times in which they were engendered; and infests society with the evils of an age, which it has left behind.

To conceive the operations which are necessary to give effect to the enactments of the legislature, it is necessary to conceive the occasions which call for them.

When the legislature has established rights, so long as there is no dispute about those rights, and so long as there is no complaint of any violation of them, so long there is no occasion for any agency to give to the enactments of the legislature their effect. The moment, however, one person says, the right to that object is mine, and another person says no, but the right to that object is mine; or the moment any man complains that such or such a right belonging to him another man has violated, that moment occasion for the agency in question begins.

It is evident, also, that the operations necessary to give effect to the enactments of the legislature are confined to those two occasions; namely, that on which a right is disputed, and that on which it has been violated. On the occasions on which a right is disputed, it is requisite to determine to whom it belongs. On the occasions on which a right has been violated, it is sometimes only required to compel reparation to the injured party; sometimes it is necessary, besides, to inflict punishment upon the offender. The question is, What are the operations required for these several results?

Where a right is disputed, all possible cases may be resolved into that of A who affirms, and B who denies. That right is mine, says A, it is not yours, says B.

The first question to be asked of A is, which, among those facts, which the legislature has determined shall give commencement to rights, happened in such a manner as to give commencement to that which is claimed as a right by him.

If no such fact is affirmed, the right does not exist. If some such fact is affirmed, it may be met by the opponent in one of two ways. B either may deny the fact, and affirm that the right never had a commencement; or he may allow the fact, and admit that the right had a commencement, but affirm that there had subsequently happened one of those facts which put an end to rights: admitting that A bought the horse, and had a right to him in the month of July, he might affirm that

A sold him again in August, and by that transaction put an end to his right.

When B meets the affirmation of A in the first way, that is, by denying the commencement of the right, he may do it in either of two ways. He may deny the investitive fact which A affirms, or not denying the fact, he may affirm some antecedent fact which deprived it of its investitive power. Thus, if A affirmed that he got the property by occupancy, B may affirm that it was not open to occupancy, but the property of another person. If A affirmed that he got the property by succession to his father, B may allow the fact of the succession, but affirm that the property did not belong to the father of A at the time of his death.

Whenever the legislature has accurately determined what are the facts which shall give commencement, and what those which shall give termination to a right, the whole confused and intricate mass of what in English law is called *Pleading*, reduces itself to these clear and simple elements. A begins, by affirming some one of the facts which gives commencement to a right. B may deny this fact directly: A affirms contract for example, B denies it; and then, of course, comes the evidence: Or, instead of denying it, B may affirm an antecedent fact which deprived the fact affirmed by A of its investitive force; or he may affirm a subsequent fact, which put an end to the right. In those two cases, in which B affirms a new fact, A must be called upon for a reply, in other words, asked whether he admits or denies it. If he admits, there is an end, of course, to the claim of A. If he denies, then again we have affirmation and denial upon a matter of fact, which is to be determined by the production of evidence.

This is the first part of the proceeding, neither intricate nor obscure. The next is, the adduction of evidence. A fact is disputed; affirmed on the one side, denied on the other. A produces evidence to prove the fact, B produces evidence to disprove it. The decision is on the one side or the other, and the dispute is at an end.

If both parties obey the decision, there is no occasion for another act. If the losing party disobeys, force is necessary to compel obedience. This is called execution, and terminates the agency required.

It is needless to particularize a penal proceeding; all the possible varieties of which fall under one or other of the cases illustrated.

Thus, when a man is charged with a crime, the prosecutor affirms one of the acts violating rights, to which punishment is annexed by the legislator. The defendant can meet this affirmation in one of only two ways. First, he may deny the act, and then the second stage of proceeding, the adduction of evidence, immediately takes place. Or, not denying the act, he may affirm some previous act, which prevented it from having the effect of violating a right. Not denying the fact of taking the horse out of the field with a view to appropriate him, he may affirm a previous purchase, gift, &c. The adduction of evidence has nothing peculiar in the case of a penal proceeding at law. In the last stage, that of execution, the peculiar act of inflicting punishment is required.

Having thus a view, though very summary, of the operations required, we shall be the better able to judge of the agents necessary for the performance.

The stages, we have observed, are three. The *first* is that in which the plaintiff adduces the fact on which he relies, and is met by the defendant either with a denial of the fact, or the affirmation of another fact, which, to maintain the suit, the plaintiff must deny. The *second* is that in which evidence, to prove or disprove the fact on which the affirmation and denial of the parties ultimately rests, is adduced and decided upon. The *third* is that in which the operations are performed necessary for giving effect to the sentence of the judge.

What is desirable in the operations of the first stage is, 1*st*, That the affirmations and negations with respect to the facts should be true; and, 2*dly*, That the facts themselves should be such as really to have the quality ascribed to them. For the first of these purposes, all the securities, which the nature of the case admits of, should be taken, for the veracity of the parties. There is the same sort of reason that the parties should speak truly, as that the witnesses should speak truly. They should speak, therefore, under all the sanctions and penalties of a witness. They cannot, indeed, in many cases swear to the existence or non-existence of the fact; which may not have been within their cognizance. But they can always swear to the state of their belief with respect to it. For the second of the above purposes, namely, that it may be known whether the facts affirmed and denied are such as to possess the quality ascribed to them, two things are necessary; the first is, that all investitive and divestitive facts and acts by which rights are violated should have been clearly predetermined by the legislature, in other words, that there should be a well-made code; the second is, that the affirmations and denials with respect to them should be made in the presence of somebody capable of telling exactly whether they have the quality ascribed to them or not. The judge is a person with this knowledge, and to him alone can the power of deciding on matters so essential to the result of the inquiry be entrusted.

To have this important part of the business done, then, in the best possible way, it is necessary that the parties should meet in the very first instance in the presence of the judge. A is asked, upon his oath, to mention the fact which he believes confers upon him or has violated his right. If it is not a fact capable of having that effect, he is told so, and his claim is at an end. If it is a fact capable of having that effect, B is asked whether he denies it; or whether he affirms another fact, either one of those, which, happening previously, would prevent it from having its imputed effect, or in a civil case one of those which, happening subsequently, would put an end to the right to which the previous fact gave commencement. If he affirmed only a fact which could have neither of these effects, the pretension of B would be without foundation.

Done in this manner, the clearness, the quickness, and the certainty of the whole proceeding are demonstrated. Remarkable it is, that every one of the rules for doing it in the best possible manner, is departed from by the English law, and that to the greatest possible extent. No security whatsoever is taken that the parties shall speak the truth; they are left with perfect impunity, aptly by Mr. Bentham denominated the *mendacity-licence,* to tell as many lies as they please. The legislature has never enumerated and defined the facts which give commencement, or put a period to or violate rights; the subject, therefore, remains in a state of confusion, obscurity, and uncertainty. And, lastly, the parties do not make their affirmations and negations before the judge, who would tell them whether the facts which they allege could or could not have the virtue ascribed to them; they make them in secret, and in writing, each along with his attorney, who has a motive to make them not in the way most conducive to the interests of his client, but in the way most conducive to his own interests, and those of his confederates, from the bottom to the top of the profession. First, A, the plaintiff, writes what is called the declaration, an instrument for the most part full of irrelevant absurdity and lies; and this he deposits in an office, where the attorney of B, the defendant, obtains a copy of it, on paying a fee. Next B, the defendant, meets the declaration of A, by what is called a plea, the form of which is not less absurd than that of the declaration. The plea is written and put into the same office, out of which the attorney of the opposite party obtains a copy of it on similar terms. The plea may be of two sorts; either, 1*st,* a dilatory plea, as it is called; or, 2*dly,* a plea to the action. To this plea the plaintiff may make a *replication,* proceeding through the same process. To the replication the defendant may put in a *rejoinder.* The plaintiff may answer the rejoinder by a *sur-rejoinder.* This, again, the defendant may oppose by a *rebutter,* and the plaintiff may answer him by a *sur-rebutter.*

All this takes place without being once seen or heard of by the judge; and no sooner has it come before him, than some flaw is perhaps discovered in it, whereupon he quashes the whole, and sends it to be performed again from the beginning.

This mischievous mess, which exists in defiance and mockery of reason, English lawyers inform us, is a strict, and pure, and beautiful exemplification of the rules of logic. This is a common language of theirs. It is a language which clearly demonstrates the state of their minds. All that they see in the system of pleading is the mode of performing it. What they know of logic is little more than the name.

The agency necessary for the performance of this portion of the business, is some person, who, when he hears a fact affirmed and denied, can tell whether it is one of those facts to which the legislature has attached the power of giving commencement or of putting a period to rights. It is evident, that on such occasion, any one person, with the requisite knowledge, attention, and probity, is as competent to the task as a hundred. If he is single, the attention and probity is likely to be the greatest, as responsibility is not weakened merely, it is almost annihilated by being shared. There should be one judge, therefore, and not more, to superintend that branch of procedure which consists of pleading.

The agency best adapted to the business of the second stage of judicature, is that which next demands our attention. It is the business of taking evidence ; in other words, the doing all that is necessary to ascertain whether the disputed fact happened or did not happen.

The subject of evidence is a matter of complexity in the detail. And where any thing complex is to be stated in words, there is always difficulty in the expression, how plain soever the ideas. Such general considerations, however, as we can even here adduce, will, we hope, throw sufficient light upon the subject, to leave no doubt with respect to the conclusions which we have it in view to establish. This is one of the topics, connected with law, which Mr. Bentham has exhausted, though a small part only of what he has written upon it has yet seen the light.*

With respect to all facts, legally operative, that is, which give or take away rights, it is desirable that evidence, amounting to proof, should, if possible, always exist. With respect to a great proportion of them, it is in the power of the legislature to take measures, that evidence of them shall be collected at the moment of their happening, and shall be preserved. This is the case with all those of which an evidentiary writing can be made and preserved by registration ; all contracts, births, deaths, marriages, and so on. The proportion is really very great of the whole number of facts, legally operative, in regard to which a legislature, by proper means, might secure the existence of evidence, and to that extent might either prevent disputes, or render the decision of them easy. That so little of this most important and obvious work has any where been done, only shows how ill the legislatures of the world have hitherto performed their duty. It is in the power of the legislature, by a proper classification, to have an accurate formulary, for the different species of *contracts, wills,* and other *evidentiary writings.* Those formularies properly made and printed with blanks to fill up, would render the business of *Conveyancing,* which, in England, is a boundless, trackless, and almost impenetrable jungle, abounding with expence, with delay and vexation to parties, with wealth and almost boundless power over the fortunes of other men to lawyers, a thing of the greatest simplicity, certainty and ease.

Into the question of what might be, and ought to be done by the legislature, for making and preserving evidence of the principal facts by which rights are made to begin or to end, we cannot enter at length, on the present occasion. The great importance which belongs to the subject, is evident from what we have thus shortly advanced.

The business of him, who is only called upon to determine whether a

---

* We are happy to say, there are hopes that this part of Mr. Bentham's writings will soon be presented to the public by M. Dumont, the first of translators and redacteurs, in that happy form which he has given to other portions of that philosopher's manuscripts.

disputed fact did or did not happen is, to make the best use of all the evidence which exists, whether it were, or were not desirable, that more had been made to exist. For the best use of that which exists, three things are necessary:

1*st*, That the whole of it should be made to bear, that is, should be taken and applied.

2*dly*, That it should be taken in those circumstances which are most conducive to trust-worthiness.

3*dly*, That the proper value should be set upon each article, and upon the whole.

1. That the evidence may be taken as completely as possible, two things are necessary. The first is, that the judge should have power to send for, and to compel the attendance of, all persons and things which may be capable of affording evidence. The second is, that the evidence should all be taken, and nothing be omitted or lost.

It is not necessary here to enter into any details with respect to the first of those requisites. The necessity of the powers is obvious, and the end to be attained is so precise and perspicuous, that there can be no difficulty in conceiving the mode of putting together and applying the means. There is no limit, it is obvious, to the physical power which should be placed at the disposal of the judge. He ought to have the right of calling upon every man, upon the whole community, to aid him in any act which is necessary to the performance of any part of his judicial duty; because any force, opposed to the performance of that duty, there ought to be a force sufficient promptly to overcome. It is convenient, however, to the community, instead of being liable to be called upon, individually, for the performance of the ordinary services auxiliary to the business of the judge, to provide him with a proper number of officers, paid for attending to execute his commands. Their principal business, as regards this stage of the judicial proceedings, is, to serve notice upon any persons whose own presence, or that of any writing or other thing which they may possess, is required by the judge. Persons or things, subjected immediately to the operations of judicature, have a particular name in English. They are said to be *forthcoming*, a word which has an exact equivalent in few other languages, and is exceedingly appropriate and useful. It is of the greatest convenience, when a concrete term, the use of which is very frequent, has an abstract term corresponding to it; as good, has goodness; hard, hardness, and so on. There was not any word in the language corresponding in this way to *forthcoming*. Mr. Bentham, perceiving the great need of it, made the term *forthcomingness;* not exceptionable on the score either of harshness or obscurity. The small wits thought proper to laugh at him. We shall, nevertheless—sorry at the same time that we cannot supply a defect in the language without offending them, make use of the word; in which we find great appropriateness and great convenience. This particular branch, therefore, of the judicial agency is that which relates to *forthcomingness;* and forthcomingness is required for two purposes, both for evidence and for justiciability; for evidence, that a true decision may be passed; for justiciability, that the sentence of the judge may not fail of its intended effect.

So much with respect to the forthcomingness of evidence. The second condition, required to give the decision the benefit of all existing evidence is, that the whole should be taken, and that not any part of it which can be taken without preponderant inconvenience should be excluded and lost.

Of the several articles of evidence, some will always be of more importance, some of less; and some may be of very little importance; but whether of little or of much, it is always desirable that all should be taken, and every the smallest portion counted for what it is worth. The discovery of truth is promoted by taking advantage of every thing which tends to throw light upon the subject of dispute.

These propositions, it may appear to be useless, indeed impertinent, formally to state. They are too evident, it may be said, to be disputed, and too important to be overlooked. Important as they are, and undisputed by all the rest of the world, they are not only disputed, but trampled upon by lawyers, especially English lawyers. They have unhappily established a set of rules in direct opposition to them. These rules they applaud in all forms of expression, and celebrate as guards and fences of all that is dear to mankind.

In all causes, they have determined, that persons so and so situated, things so and so situated, though apt to be pregnant with information beyond all other persons and things, shall not be admitted as sources of evidence. Thus, in English law, we have incompetency of witnesses, that is, exclusion of them, 1*st*, From want of understanding; 2*dly*, From defect of religious principle; 3*dly*, From infamy of character; 4*thly*, From interest. These are undisguised modes of exclusion; besides which, there is an extensive assortment of disguised modes. Under this title comes the rule, that only the best evidence be given which the nature of the case admits of; according to which, it often happens that the only evidence which can be had is excluded. Under this title also falls the rule, making certain kinds of evidence conclusive, by which proceeding, all other evidence is excluded. To the same list belongs the rule, that hearsay evidence is not admissible. The rules, so extensive in their application, by which writings are wholly rejected, only because they want certain formularies, are rules of exclusion; and so are the limitations with respect to time, and to number of witnesses. Into the very extensive subject, however, of the absurdity and mischievousness of the rules of evidence in English law, we cannot pretend so much as to enter. A remarkable exemplification of them was afforded on the trial of Warren Hastings, to which, for this purpose, the reader may be referred. (See Mill's *History of British India*, Book VI. Chap. ii.)

The only conceivable reasons for the exclusion of evidence are three:
1. Irrelevancy.
2. Inconvenience in obtaining and producing.

3. Danger of deception.

With regard to irrelevancy the decision is clear. What has no tendency either to prove or disprove the point in question, it would be loss of time to receive.

With regard to inconvenience, it is no doubt liable to happen, that when all the good which can be expected from the obtaining of a lot of evidence is compared with the evil of the delay, cost, and vexation, inseparable from the obtaining of it, the evil may be more than an overmatch for the good. In all such cases, it is expedient that the lot of evidence should be foregone.

As a guard against the danger of deception, it is equally certain that no evidence ought ever to be excluded. An account of all the reasons by which the absurdity is demonstrated of exclusion on this ground, and of the wide and deplorable mischief which, in the vulgar systems, is produced by it, would be far too extensive for the contracted limits of the present discourse. Reasons, however, decisive of the question, present themselves so obviously, that hardly any man, with an ordinary understanding, not fettered by prejudice, can look at the subject without perceiving them.

If evidence is to be received from no source from which evidence, liable to produce deception, is capable of coming, evidence must not be received at all. Evidence must be received from sources whence false evidence, as well as true, is liable to flow. To refuse all information from such sources, is not the way by which a knowledge of the truth can be obtained. This is the way to make sure of not having that knowledge. The means of obtaining it are, to receive evidence from every possible source, and to separate the bad from the good, under all those securities, and by the guidance of all those marks, of which understanding and attention know how to avail themselves.

It is not enough to say, we will receive information from those sources only which are least likely to yield deceptious evidence, refuse to receive it from those which are most likely. You are obliged to receive it from sources differing in almost all possible degrees of likelihood. Where are you to draw the line of separation? Is not the same discernment which guards you against the danger of false information from the sources which you deem the least likely to yield it, sufficient to guard you against it from those sources which you deem the most likely to do so? In fact it will be still more sufficient; because in this case you will be much more apt to be upon your guard. The very best information is, in truth, liable to be derived from the very worst of sources,—from a man who, you know, would not tell you one word of truth, if he could help it.

The securities that a man will give true information, independently of those artificial securities which the legislature can apply equally to all, are, 1*st*, Intelligence, 2*dly*, Probity, 3*dly*, Freedom from interest. Suppose that one, or two, or all of these securities are wanting; it only follows, that what he states should be heard with a proportional distrust. It may still be of the utmost importance to the discovery of the truth that he should be heard. Hear him with the proper allowances, and it must always be less favourable to that great end, that, he should not be heard at all. His testimony may appear, when heard, to be utterly unworthy of credence. But that could not be known till it was heard and examined. It might so have been, that it was not only worthy of credence, but completed the proof of a fact of the greatest possible importance. That a man should not be heard as a witness, on account of his religious creed, is an absurdity which we cannot descend to notice.

2. The second of the three things which we found necessary, as above, for making the best use judicially of whatever evidence, to the fact in question, exists, was, that it should be taken under those circumstances, which are most conducive to trust-worthiness. Those circumstances are constituted by the artificial securities, which arrangements can be made to apply. The following enumeration of them has been made by Mr. Bentham *(Introduction to the Rationale of Evidence,* p. 54), and appears to be complete.

1. Punishment.
2. Shame.
3. Interrogation, including counter-interrogation.
4. Counter evidence,—admission of.
5. Writing,—use made of it for giving permanence, &c. to evidence.
6. Publicity,—to most purposes and on most occasions.
7. Privacy,—to some purposes, and on some occasions.

For developing the import of these several securities, we can afford to say nothing. The principal operation of the judicial functionary in this part of the business is, to preside over the interrogation; to see that it is properly and completely performed. The question, then, what is the sort of agency best adapted for the performance of this part of the task of taking evidence is not difficult to answer. There is nothing in it which one man, with the proper intellectual and moral qualifications, is not as capable of performing, as any number of men.

3. All the existing evidence being collected and received, it only remains that the proper value should be attached to the several portions, and a corresponding decision pronounced.

It is sufficiently evident that, for the performance of this duty, no very precise instructions can be laid down. The value which belongs to an article of evidence often depends on minute and almost indescribable circumstances; and the result must be left to the sagacity and conscience of the judge.

At the same time, however, service to this end, and of the greatest importance, may be, and, of course, ought to be, rendered by the legislature. The different marks of trust-worthiness may, to a certain extent of particularity, be very correctly described. This being done, the difference between the value of any two lots of evidence, to which those marks attach, may be very exactly ascertained. One has a certain number of the marks of trust-worthiness, as laid down by the legislature; another has all these and so many more; the result is clear. It is evident, that as far, in this respect, as experience and foresight can go, nothing should be left undone by the legislature.

Another important service can be rendered by the legislature; and that is, to provide an accurate language for the judge; a language in which he can express precisely the degree of value which he allots to each article of evidence, and to the whole. Various expedients may be adopted for this purpose. A very obvious one is, to fix upon some particular, well known, article of evidence, the value of which all men appreciate equally; the clear testimony, for example, of a man of the ordinary degree of intelligence and probity, as a standard. Is the value to be expressed, which the judge attaches to any other article of evidence? If inferior to the standard, it falls below it by so many degrees, one, two, three, four: If superior, it rises above it by so many.

Having provided an accurate language, the legislature should take security that it be used; and admit of no vague and general expressions in the account of the value which the judge attaches to each article of the evidence on which he grounds his decision.

At the same time that the legislature insists upon the use of precise language in stating the value of evidence, it should insist upon reasons; upon receiving from the judge a precise statement of the grounds upon which he attaches such a value, and no other, to each and every article of evidence; that is, upon receiving a reference, as exact as language can give, to each of the circumstances which contributed to suggest to him that particular estimate which he says he has formed.

Of the importance of all these expedients we presume that no illustration is required.

We come now to the third and last stage of the business of judicature; when all that remains is to carry into effect the sentence of the judge.

When they, upon whom the sentence operates, are willing to obey, all that is necessary is, to afford them notice of what it requires them to perform. In well ordered countries, all but a very insignificant number will be found to be cases of this description. When opposition is to be overcome, a physical force must be provided, sufficient for the purpose. As there seems nothing mysterious in determining how this should be formed, and under what rules it should act, to secure the ends for which it is provided, with the smallest possible amount of collateral evil, we shall here take leave of the subject.

VII.

The Judicial Establishment; or Inquiry what is the best form of the Agency required for giving effect to the Laws.—Securities for the intellectual Endowments of the Judge.—Securities for the moral Qualities of the Judge.

We have now seen the whole of the operations to be performed. The parties are received to state before the judge the investitive or divestitive facts on which they rely. If they state, for this purpose, a fact which is not possessed of those qualities, they are immediately told that it is not possessed of them, and not calculated to support their claim. They come, by two, or three steps, at the longest, to a fact upon which the question ultimately turns; and which is either contested, or not contested. In a great many cases it would not be contested. When the subject was stript of disguise, the party who had no right, would generally see that he had no hope, and would acquiesce. The suit would thus be terminated without the adduction of evidence. When it was not, the cases would be frequent in which it might be terminated by the evidence which the parties brought along with them. In these cases, also, the first hearing would suffice. A vast majority of the whole number of suits would be included in these two sets of cases. For the decision of a vast majority, therefore, of the whole number of suits, a few minutes would suffice. When all the evidence could not be forthcoming at the first hearing, and only then, would a second hearing be required. In this mode of proceeding, justice would be, that without which it is not justice, expeditious and cheap.

In all this there is nothing which one man, with the appropriate intellectual and moral qualities, is not as competent to perform as any number of men. As one man is cheaper than any greater number, that is one reason why no more than one judge should be allowed to one tribunal.

The next object of inquiry is, to ascertain what securities can be provided that those who are entrusted with the business of judicature shall possess the requisite intellectual and moral endowments.

The intellectual endowments depend upon those who have the power of choosing and of dismissing the judges: and who do or do not appoint men whose knowledge and capacity are ascertained. The moral behaviour of the judges depends upon the interests which act upon them in the situation in which they are placed.

Into the question, who should have the appointment of the judges, we do not intend to enter. The answer would be different under different forms of government; and this is not the place to compare the different forms of government, either for this or any other of the ends of its institution. One thing only we shall state, because it carries its evidence along with it. Those who appoint the judges ought to have no interest contrary to the best administration of justice.

As the uprightness of the judge is assailed by interests inseparable from his situation; viz. the profit which he may derive from misdecision, it is necessary to counterbalance them by opposite interests, assuming the character of securities. Several of the securities, which we have already seen applying to the situation of witness, apply also to the situation of judge: Some are peculiar to each. The following is the list of those which apply to the situation of judge.
1. Punishment.
2. Shame.
3. Publicity.
4. Writing, for the sake of accuracy and permanence.
5. Singleness of the functionary.
6. Appeal.

For the *Punishment* of the several kinds of judicial offences, provision ought to be made in the penal code.

In the case of the judge there is particular occasion to point accurately, and to strengthen to the utmost, the operation of *Shame;* for in the situation of judge it is possible to be guilty of offences very numerous and very serious, without permitting so much of evidence to attach to any definite act, as would suffice to form a ground for punishment.

The great instrument for the application of shame is *Publicity.* The importance of publicity, therefore, is paramount. It is not only the great instrument for creating and applying the moral sanction, the approbation and disapprobation of mankind; but it is of essential service towards the application of punishment, by making known the occasions on which it is deserved. It is not only a great security in itself, but it is the principle of life and strength to all other securities.

All other publicity is feeble and of little worth compared with that of the *Press.* Not only, therefore, ought this to be allowed to operate with its utmost force upon the judge, but effectual provision ought to be made to cause it to operate upon him with its utmost force. Not only ought the judgment hall to be rendered as convenient as possible for the reception of the public; not only ought the greatest freedom to be enjoyed in publishing the proceedings of the judge; and in publishing all manner of observations upon them, favourable or unfavourable; but measures ought to be taken to make a public, and to produce publication, where there is any chance that a voluntary public, and voluntary publication, would be wanting. For this purpose, unless other very important considerations intervene, the judgment seat should always be in that place, within the district to which it belongs, where the most numerous and intelligent public, and the best means of publication, are to be had.

In England, where there is no definition of libel, and where the judges, therefore, are allowed to punish, under the name of libel, whatever writing they do not like, the publishing of unfavourable observations on the conduct of a judge—nay, in some instances, and these the highest in importance, the simple report of his proceedings—is treated as one of the most heinous of all possible offences. No wonder! Allow judges, or allow any men, to frame laws, and they will frame them, if they can, to answer their own purposes. Who would not, if he could, make a law to protect himself from censure? More especially if he were a man disposed to act in such a way as to deserve censure?

Would you allow falsehood to be published against the judge? The word falsehood is here ambiguous. It means both erroneous opinions, and false statements with regard to fact. Erroneous opinions we would undoubtedly permit, because we know no standard for ascertaining them, other than that which is afforded by public discussion; and because this is an adequate remedy for all the evil which erroneous opinions have any tendency to produce. Affirmation of facts injurious to the judge, if false, and made without reasonable grounds for having been believed to be true, we would prevent.

Allow facts, injurious to the judge, to be published, even when true; allow comments, unfavourable to the judge, to be made upon his actions, you discredit the administration of justice. Discredit the administration of justice, to which the people are resorting every day for the greatest of all possible benefits, protection from injury! As well talk of discrediting the business of a bread-baker, a meat-seller, if the fraudulent dealer is exposed to the censures of the public! Discredit the administration of justice, indeed, by taking measures of security against the vices of judges, indispensable for its perfection!

The importance of *recording, in permanent characters,* what takes place before the judge, we must content ourselves with assuming. We may do so, it is presumed, with propriety, on account of the facility with which the reasons present themselves. We must also leave it to our readers to draw the line of distinction between the occasions on which it is requisite, and the occasions on which it may be dispensed with; the occasions, for example, where every thing is simple and clear, and all parties are satisfied.

It is a great security, both for diligent and for upright conduct in the judge, that he occupy *singly* the judgment seat. When a man knows that the whole credit and reward of what is done well; the whole punishment and disgrace of what is done ill, will belong to himself, the motive to good conduct is exceedingly increased. When a man hopes that he can shuffle off the blame of negligence, the blame of unfairness, or fix a part of it on another, the uncertainty of the punishment operates, as we have already seen, to the diminution, and almost to the extinction, of its preventive force. Certain common, and even proverbial expressions, mark the general experience of that indifference, with which a duty, that belongs in common to many, is apt to be performed. What is every body's business is nobody's. This is as true in the family as in the state ; as true in judicature as in ordinary life. Much remains to be said upon this topic, which is one of great importance ; but we must pass to the next.

Of the use of *appeal*, as a security against the misconduct of the judge, there is the less occasion to adduce any proof, because it seems to be fully recognized by the practice of nations.

One thing, however, which is not recognized by that practice, is, that, if it is necessary in any one sort of causes, so it is in every other, without exception. Not a single reason can be given why it should exist in one set of cases, which is not equally strong to prove that it should exist in any other.

It is instructive to observe the cases in which it has been supposed that it ought to exist, and the cases in which it has been supposed that it might be omitted. The cases in which it has been thought necessary, are those which concern property of considerable value. Those in which it has been dispensed with are those which concern property of inconsiderable value. The first set of cases are those which are of importance to the aristocratical class ; the second are those which are of no importance to that class. It is the aristocratical class who have made the laws ; they have accordingly declared that the suits which were important to them should have the benefit of appeal; the suits not important to them should not have the benefit of appeal.

We recognize only one standard of importance; namely, influence upon human happiness and misery. The small sum of money for which the suit of the poor man is instituted is commonly of much greater importance to him, than the larger sum for which the suit of the rich man is instituted is to the rich. Again, for one rich man there are thousands and thousands of poor. In the calculation, then, of perfect benevolence, the suits for the small sums are not, as in the calculation of perfect aristocracy, those of the least, or rather no importance; they are of ten thousand times greater importance than the suits for the largest sums.

If an appeal ought to be had, how many *stages* should there be of appeal ? This question, we imagine, is easily answered. If you go for a second judgment, you should, if possible, go to the very best source: and if you go at once to the best source, why go any farther ?

What is required to be done, in the case of an appeal, is the first thing which deserves to be ascertained. An appeal takes place in consequence of a complaint against the previous judge. Where no complaint, there is no appeal, nor place for appeal.

A complaint against the judge must relate to his conduct, either at the first, the second, or the third stage, of the judicial operations.

If to his conduct at the first stage, it must be a complaint of his having permitted a party to rest upon a fact which had not the investitive or divestitive quality ascribed to it; and this implies either a mistake with respect to the law, or that he allowed the decision to turn upon a fact which did not embrace the merits of the question. It is evident, that for the decision of this question, all that is necessary is an exact transcription of *the pleadings*, and transmission of them to the court of appeal.

If the complaint relates to his conduct at the second stage, it must turn upon one of two points; either that he did not take all the evidence, or that he did not properly determine its value.

If he did not take the evidence properly, by a failure either in assembling the sources of it, or in extracting it from them when assembled, the proper remedy is to send back the cause to him, with an order to him to supply the omission; or, if he be suspected of having failed wilfully, to send it to the judge of one of the neighbouring districts, to retake the evidence and decide.

If the complaint relates to a wrong estimate of the evidence, the statement of it, transmitted to the court of appeal, with the reasons assigned by the judge for the value affixed to every portion of it, will enable the appellate court to decide.

With regard to the third stage, the only complaint there can be is, that the judge has not taken measures to execute his own sentence. If any inquiry is in this case to be made, the proper course is, that the appellate court refer it to one of the neighbouring judges. When a simple act is to be done, the proper order is to be dispatched, and the proper penalties for non-performance exacted.

It thus appears, that for every thing which is required to be done by the appellate judicature, nothing whatsoever is required, as a foundation, but certain papers. The presence is not required, either of parties or of witnesses.

As it is of no great consequence, in a country in which the means of communication are tolerably provided, whether papers have to be transmitted 50 or 500 miles, the distance, even though considerable, of the seat of the appellate jurisdiction is a matter of very little importance. The object, then, is to get the best seat; that is, the best public. The best public, generally speaking, is in the capital. The capital, then, is the proper seat of all appellate jurisdiction. And that there should be one judge, and one judge only, in each court of appeal, is proved by exactly the same reasons, as those which apply to the courts of primary jurisdiction.

The question how many courts there should be, as well of primary as of appellate jurisdiction, is to be determined by one thing, and one thing only; namely, the need there is for them. The number of the courts of primary jurisdiction must be determined, in some instances, by the number of suits; in some, by local extent. To render justice sufficiently accessible, the distance from the seat of judicature must not be great, though the number of accruing suits, either from the paucity or from the good conduct of the people, should be ever so small.

As the judgment seat should never be empty, for the need of staying injustice is not confined to times and seasons, and as one judge may be sometimes ill, sometimes called to a distance even by the duties of his office, provision ought to be made for supplying his place. For this purpose the proper expedient is a deputy. That the deputy should well perform his duty, the best security is, that he should be chosen and employed by the judge, the judge being responsible for the acts of the deputy, as his own. Whatever it be, which the judge cannot do, or cannot conveniently do, in that he may employ his deputy. If there is a great influx of causes, the deputy may be employed in some of the least complex and difficult. If there is any business, not of first-rate importance, requiring the presence of the judge at a distance, the delegation of the deputy or deputies is the proper resource.

Besides the judge and his deputy, there are two adjuncts to every tribunal, which are of the utmost importance; indispensable, indeed, to the due administration of justice. These are, a *pursuer-general,* and a *defender-general.* The business of both pursuer-general, and defender-general is, to reclaim the execution of all laws in the execution of which the nation has a peculiar interest, though individuals may not. The peculiar business of the pursuer-general is, to act on behalf of the administrative authority, in its character of plaintiff, and on behalf of every plaintiff who is without the means of engaging another advocate; to obviate any prejudice he sees likely to arise to justice from the conduct of plaintiffs, whether in civil matters or penal; and to perform, in the case of all offences, where no private prosecutor appears, the office of prosecutor. The peculiar duty of the defender-general is, to act on behalf of the administrative authority in its capacity of defendant, and on behalf of every defendant who has not the means of engaging another advocate, and to obviate any prejudice he sees likely to result to justice from want of skill or other causes on the part of a defendant who pleads his own cause, or on the part of the advocate who pleads it for him.

The courts of appeal, though all seated in the metropolis, ought to be as numerous as the speedy hearing of all the appeals which come to them requires. The judges of appeal ought all to be chosen from the judges of primary jurisdiction, not only on account of the education and the experience received, but as a step of promotion, and a proper motive to acquire the requisite education, and to merit approbation in the inferior employment. There is the same propriety, and for the same reason, in choosing the judges of primary jurisdiction from the deputies.

(F. F.)

THE ARTICLE

LIBERTY OF THE PRESS,

REPRINTED FROM

THE SUPPLEMENT

TO THE

ENCYCLOPÆDIA BRITANNICA.

LIBERTY OF THE PRESS.

I.

Nature and Objects of the Inquiry.

THE task of pointing out which of the acts, capable of being committed by the press, it would be expedient to prohibit under penalties, we trust will be found to be greatly diminished, by what we have already established in the articles GOVERNMENT and JURISPRUDENCE.

There is scarcely a right, for the violation of which, scarcely an operation of government, for the disturbance of which the press may not be employed as an instrument. The offences capable of being committed by the press are indeed nearly co-extensive with the whole field of delinquency.

It is not, however, necessary to give a separate definition of every such violation or disturbance, when committed by the press; for that would be to write the penal code a second time; first describing each offence as it appears in ordinary cases; and then describing it anew for the case in which the press is the particular instrument.

If, for the prevention of the violation of rights, it were necessary to give a separate definition, on account of every instrument which might be employed as a means of producing the several violations, the penal code would be endless. In general, the instrument or means is an immaterial circumstance. The violation itself, and the degree of alarm which may attend it, are the principle objects of consideration. If a man is put in fear of his life, and robbed of his purse, it is of no consequence whether he is threatened with a pistol or with a sword. In the definition of a theft, of a fraud, or a murder, it is not necessary to include an account of all the sorts of means by which these injuries may be perpetrated. It is sufficient if the injury itself is accurately described. The object is to prevent the injury, not merely when produced by one sort of means or another sort of means, but by any means.

From these illustrations, it sufficiently appears, that, if an accurate penal code were composed, defining the violations of rights, and the disturbances of the operations of government, to which penalties were to be annexed, every offence, capable of being committed by the press, would be defined without mentioning the press. It is no less evident, that if we include in the term *libel*, as, to the great encouragement of confusion, is generally done, all the offences capable of being committed by the press, we include in the definition of libel all the definitions of the penal code.

As far as Persons and Property are concerned, the general definition of the acts by which rights are liable to be violated, has always been held sufficient; and has been regarded as including not less the cases in which the instrumentality of the press has been employed, than those in which any other means have been employed to the same end. Nobody ever thought of a particular law for restraining the press on account of the cases in which it may have been rendered subservient to the perpetration of a murder or a theft. It is enough that a law is made to punish him who has been guilty of the murder or theft, whether he has employed the press or any thing else as the means for accomplishing his end.

There can be no doubt, however, that the press is an instrument peculiarly adapted for the commission of injuries against Reputation, and for effecting disturbance to the operations of Government, while it has no peculiar adaptation for the commission of other offences. Here, too, there is the greatest disposition to restrain the press within improper limits. It is demanded of us, therefore, upon this part of the subject, to enter into greater detail.

We are then to inquire, in the first place, what are the acts of the press with respect to *private reputation?* and next, what are the acts with respect to *government*, which it is desirable that punishment should be employed to restrain?

II.

Offences of the Press with respect to Private Rights.

Agreeably to the principles which have been already considered in the article JURISPRUDENCE, no act can be regarded as an offence with respect to an individual, which is not a violation of some of his rights.*

In considering the rights which ought to be established with respect to reputation, one proposition may be assumed; That every man should be considered as having a right to the character which he deserves; that is, to be spoken of according to his actions.

Such Offences should be defined.

In what manner the definition of this right, which would form a part

* In the description which follows of that violation of rights which is most liable to be committed by the press, and of the mode in which it ought to be treated, the developements presented in the article JURISPRUDENCE are understood to be in the mind of the reader; if they are not, the very brief exposition here given will not be understood.

of the civil code, should be expressed, is not now the question; it is evident there is no peculiar difficulty in the matter. As words, not thoughts, are the object of legal cognizance, the right can only have respect to security against certain words; words, imputing to the individual, actions which he has not performed, or a disposition to certain actions, without evidence that such a disposition exists.

Suppose that one man has instituted a suit against another, for the offence of having violated, through the press, his right to some part of the reputation which he deserves. In his ground of complaint he must affirm that the man has imputed to him either the performance of actions which he did not commit, or a disposition to certain actions, where no evidence of such disposition can be given.

The words are produced; and the first question is, whether they do or do not impute the actions which, in the complaint, or bill of accusation, they are alleged to impute?

It is to be observed, that they who oppose the attempt to define the offences, which, for shortness, we call the offences of the press, make use of such occasions, as this, to raise their objections. How, they ask, can all the forms of expression be defined, by which the imputation of such and such actions may be, either more openly, or more covertly, conveyed?

It is very evident that the question, on such an occasion, whether the words do or do not impute such or such actions, is a question of fact. The law says, that such and such actions shall not be imputed, defining the actions. Whether such and such a man has imputed such actions, and whether by one set of words, or another set of words, are questions of fact.

The law, when it said that such and such acts should not be imputed to a man, could not determine whether A, who is accused by B, of having imputed to him one of those acts, did so, or not. That is to be determined by evidence, bearing upon the point. One, and in general the main article of that evidence, are the words which have been used. What is the import of these words; or, which comes to the same thing, what is the degree of proof involved in them, is to be determined, as all questions respecting the weight of evidence are, in each instance, to be determined, by the tribunal before which the accusation is brought. The interpretation of words rests upon the same footing in this, as in all other cases, that, for example, of a Will. The law determines, that whatsoever disposition a man has made with respect to his property, shall take effect after his death. But whether A has left his manor of Dale to B, is a matter of fact to be determined by evidence applying to that particular point; principally by that arising from the words of the will.

It may still be argued, by persons who do not easily renounce an opinion to which they have once given their support, that the actions, the imputation of which, the legislature means to prohibit, cannot be defined.

But this is a position which cannot long be maintained.

It is hurtful to a man, if he is believed to have committed some actions, or to have a disposition to commit them; it is not hurtful in the case of others. Evidently it is by imputation of the first sort alone, that any right with respect to reputation can be infringed.

The acts, which a man receives injury from being believed to have committed, or to be disposed to commit, are either those to which the law has annexed penalties, or those to which the penalties of public disrepute and dislike are annexed.

With respect to those acts to which the law has annexed penalties, as theft, murder, perjury, and so on, it will not be pretended that there is any difficulty; the law has already defined them, or ought to define them, and they may be marked with perfect precision by a few words.

Those acts which it is hurtful to a man, solely on account of the disrepute and dislike which they produce, to have it believed that he has committed them, may also be with sufficient accuracy determined.

Compensation should be made to the individual for injuries sustained by Offences of the Press.

The ends to be attained by punishment are, Reparation to the individual to whom injury has been done, and Prevention of similar acts in future.

In the idea of all punishment, effectual reparation to the injured individual is a necessary and essential ingredient. Suppose, then, it were declared by the legislature, that every imputation to a man of acts which bring the evil of dislike and disrepute upon him who has committed them, that is, every false imputation, shall be punished at least by reparation to be made to the party injured; the term *evil* is to this purpose perfectly precise. It would remain with the complainant to show what kind and degree of injury he had received; which is a matter of fact, to be estimated, in each instance, from the evidence adduced, by the tribunal before which the question is brought. If the injury sustained is a pecuniary injury, the question coincides exactly with the question of damages, decided regularly, in English courts, as a question of fact, by the jury.

Injuries of the kind which we are now considering can affect a man only in two ways; either, by lessening the pecuniary value which he might otherwise have enjoyed; or, by lessening the marks of respect and affection which he would otherwise have received. What the loss is, in this latter instance, is also evidently a question of fact. It has nothing, therefore, to do with the legal definition of the offence, the business of the legislature. It is a question, which, like all other questions of fact, must of necessity be determined upon evidence by the tribunal before which it is brought. It is no doubt a question of delicacy, and considerable difficulty, because the evidence must often consist of very fine and minute circumstances, which can seldom be precisely ascertained. But this is not the only class of judicial questions, the determination of which depends upon such evidence as it is very difficult accurately to collect and to weigh. What is of greatest importance, on this occasion, to remark is, that all the difficulty lies in the matter of fact. There is no doubt or obscurity in the law, which says, that whatsoever hurt a man has sustained through actions or dispositions falsely imputed to him, he shall receive compensation for. Difficulties, however, arising either from the complexity of the matter of fact, or the obscurity of the evidence, no legislative enactments can prevent. These are confided to the skill and integrity of the judge.

The compensation which ought to be made to a man for the diminution of those marks of respect and affection which he would otherwise have received, is a question for the legislature. Let us suppose that a soldier has been accused of cowardice, in such a manner as to create a general belief of the truth of the accusation; that a man of honour has been accused of mendacity, or of some of those irregular propensities to which the horror of the public is attached; it is evident that money is not, in such cases, an appropriate compensation.

When a man, through the offence of another, has been deprived of a certain amount of money, or of money's worth, we say that he has received compensation, when he is placed in the same situation in which he would have been, if the offence had never taken place.

According to this idea of compensation, a man, against whom an unfavourable opinion has been created, by the act of another man, has received compensation, when he is placed in the same situation with regard to the opinion of those with whom he is connected, as if that act had not taken place. This, therefore, is the object which it ought to be the endeavour of the legislature to effect.

One expedient is perfectly appropriate. It is, that the man who has falsely propagated an unfavourable opinion with respect to another, should be made to do whatever is in his power to remove the impression he has made. To this end, he should publish the sentence of the judge, declaring that the action, or disposition which he had imputed to the individual injured, he had imputed to him falsely. He should at least be made to publish it in every way in which he had published the imputation. Frequently a more extensive publication might be required.

In most cases, it will be allowed, that thus much would suffice. It may, however, be affirmed, that often the impression would be too profoundly struck, to be effaced by a mere knowledge of the sentence of the judge. In such cases, something more in the way of compensation would be required. On this, it is of importance to be observed, that if the impression produced by an imputation, which, after solemn inquiry, the judge has declared to be false, should not, by that declaration, be completely effaced, it implies necessarily one of two things; either that the public have evidence of the truth of the accusation, which was not adduced to the judge, and then the remaining impression is not owing to the imputation which the judge has condemned, but to the evidence; or, secondly, that the public mind is in a state of gross ignorance and imbecility, capable of forming opinions, even on the clearest subjects, not only not according to evidence, but in opposition to it. If the public mind, however, is in such a deplorable condition, it is the fault of the legislature; and for the rectification of this evil, the best course undoubtedly is, to take effectual measures for the instruction of the people, which instruction would soon place them beyond the danger of such delusions. In the mean time, if something more than the publication of the sentence of the judge were necessary to restore a man to that degree of consideration, of which the false imputation had deprived him, governments have numerous ways of raising the consequence of individuals; and no legislature would be at a loss for a gradation of expedients suited to the scale of demand.

Means which should be used for preventing the violation of Rights by the Press.

We have now illustrated that part of this question which regards compensation to the injured individual. It remains to inquire what is best to be done in this case, for the attainment of the other object of punishment, namely, the prevention of similar offences in time to come.

To devise a punishment sufficient to prevent an offence, is to provide a motive sufficient to counteract the motive which leads to the offence. We have hence to consider what are the motives by which men are incited to make false imputations on the characters of others.

These motives may be of three different sorts. A man may derive *pecuniary profit*, he may derive *comparative distinction*, or he may satisfy his desire of *vengeance*, by blackening the character of his neighbour.

In the case in which a man has by calumny wrongfully intercepted the pecuniary receipts of his neighbour, the obligation of making satisfaction to the party injured would, it is obvious, alone suffice, provided the machinery of the laws were sufficiently perfect, to render the execution of them certain. Seldom would any man calumniate his neighbour, for the sake of placing £20 in his own pocket, if he were sure that, next day, or next week, he would have to restore it, with all the profit which might have been made by the use of it, and with the disgrace besides of having committed an action which other men abhor.

Sometimes, however, a man may derive pecuniary profit from calumniating persons whom he has not by that means deprived of any pecuniary advantage; by the sale, for example, of a slanderous publication; when the satisfaction due to the individual may not be of a nature to counteract the motive which leads to the offence. The expedient in this case, also, is sufficiently obvious, and sufficiently simple. It is necessary to ascertain the whole of the gain which has been made by the offender, and to take it away from him. This, together with the satisfaction which he ought to make to the injured individual, would, if it were certain, create a surplus of motive to abstain from the injurious act.

In both of these cases, if the execution of the law is uncertain, an additional punishment may be necessary, sufficient to compensate for the chance of escape. The allowance to be made on this score must depend upon the imperfection of the laws; while one important fact is to be kept in remembrance, that as a severity of punishment, beyond a certain point, is increased, certainty of execution is diminished. The true expedient, therefore, is to render the machinery of the laws so perfect, that the penalties which they denounce may always be sure of execution; and then hardly any thing beyond compensation to the individual, and the abstraction of any additional gain which might have been made by the propagation of slander, would be necessary to repress all offences against the reputation of others, to which the motive was constituted by pecuniary gain.

The two remaining cases are still more simple. If a man propagates a falsehood, for the sake of injuring the character of a man by whom his own consideration is eclipsed, it is only when he expects to obtain by that means a permanent advantage. If he knows that immediately the law will take its hold upon him; that he will be compelled to re-elevate the character of his neighbour, and to proclaim his own disgrace, he will see that, to attempt depressing the character of another man by calumny, is the very worst of all expedients, for giving a comparative elevation to his own. The same is the result in the case where vengeance constitutes the motive to injure the reputation of another. To render this proposition manifest, the most obvious illustration will suffice. No man, to gratify his malignity to another person, would kill his ox or his ass, provided he were sure that immediately he would be obliged to make him full satisfaction; and instead of injuring the man whom he hated, to injure only himself. No, the rudeness and inefficacy of the law, holding out a chance of escaping the duty of making reparation, is the sole origin and cause of all offences of this description; and if the law were placed in a state but approaching perfection, hardly any thing beside the obligation of making satisfaction would be necessary to repress the whole of this order of crimes.

Whether any Imputation by which Truth is not violated, should be considered an Offence by the Press.

We have now made considerable progress in this important inquiry. We have ascertained, we think, with sufficient evidence, all that is necessary to be done for preventing injuries to the reputation of individuals; provided the rights of reputation are, by the civil code, not made to extend beyond the boundaries of truth. Whether or not they ought to extend farther, and individuals ought to be protected from the disclosure of acts which they may have committed, is, we confess, a question highly worthy of solution; upon which, therefore, before we proceed to any of the subsequent topics, we shall offer the following reflections.

There can be no doubt that the feelings of the individual may be as painful, where actions of a disreputable nature are, truly, as where they are falsely, imputed to him. It is equally certain, that no painful feelings ought to be wilfully excited in any man, where no good, sufficient to overbalance hat evil, is its natural consequence.

We have already shown, that reputation is injured by the imputation of acts of two different descriptions; first, those to which the law annexes penalties; secondly, those to which disrepute and the dislike of others are annexed.

With respect to those acts to which the law annexes penalties, there is no room for uncertainty or dispute. Unless the law is a bad law, which ought to be repealed (this, we confess, constitutes an exception, and one, which, in very imperfect codes, extends a great way), the law ought not to be disappointed of its execution. The man who gives information against a murderer, or a thief, by the press, or without the press, renders a public service, and deserves not punishment but reward.

It appears, therefore, that the question, whether a man ought to be protected from the imputation of actions which he has really committed, refers solely to those acts which, without being punishable by the law, are attended with disrepute; acts, in other words, which the members of the society disapprove and dislike.

The prospect of the immediate and public exposure of all acts of this description, would be a most effectual expedient to prevent their being committed. Men would obtain the habit of abstaining from them, and would feel it as little painful to abstain, as at present it is to any well educated person to keep from theft, or those acts which constitute the ill manners of the vulgar. The fable of Momus has always been understood to carry an important moral. He found grievous fault that a window had not been placed in the breast of every man, by which, not his actions alone, but his thoughts, might have been known. The magnanimity of that Roman has been highly applauded, who not only placed his residence in such a situation that his fellow-citizens might see as much as possible of his actions, but declared a wish that he could open to all eyes his breast as well as his house.

If the hatred and contempt of the people, therefore, were always rightly directed, and rightly proportioned; if they never operated against any actions but those which were hurtful, either to the individual himself, or to others, and never, but in the degree in which they were hurtful, the case would be clear; the advantage which would be derived from the true exposure of any man's actions of any sort, would exceed beyond calculation the attendant evil. The great difficulty of insuring the practice of morality, in those numerous and highly important cases, to which the legal sanction, or the *security of pains and penalties* does not extend, consists in the want of a motive always present, and powerful enough to counteract the instant motive which urges to the instant offence. That motive almost every man would derive from the knowledge that he had the eyes upon him of all those, the good opinion of whom it was his interest to preserve; that no immoral act of his would escape their observation, and a proportionate share of their hatred and contempt. It is in this view that the aid of religion has been sometimes regarded as of importance to morality; suggesting the idea of a high and constant observer. All motives, however, are feeble, in proportion as the pains and pleasures upon which they depend are distant, vague, or uncertain. Divines agree with all other men in complaining of the trifling effect of religious motives upon the lives of the greater number of men. From the nature of the prospect on which these motives depend, they could not be less feeble than they have been thus described. The case is not the same with the motives arising from the sentiments which we know we shall inspire in the breasts of our fellow-creatures. It is a matter of daily and incontrovertible experience, that these are among the most powerful which operate upon the human mind. The soldier rushes upon death, and endures all the hardships and toils of his cruel profession, that he may enjoy the admiration, and escape the contempt of his fellow men. On what else is founded the greater part of all human pursuits? How few, even of those who toil at the meanest occupations, but exert themselves to have something for show, something to make an impression upon the eyes of those who surround them? The very subject of the present inquiry derives from this source the whole of its importance. The value of reputation is, indeed, but another name for the value which we attach to the favourable and unfavourable sentiments of our fellow men.

It is, however, true, that their unfavourable sentiments do not always fall where they ought, and this, we confess, is a consideration of the highest importance. It very often happens that men's antipathies are excited to actions from which no evil ensues, either to him who performs them, or to any body else. If any man derives a pleasure from such actions, it is to limit his sphere of innocent enjoyment, to debar him from them. And if the press exposes him to the antipathies, the hatred, and contempt of his fellow-creatures, on account of those actions, it produces an evil, uncompensated by the smallest portion of good. To an Indian Brahmen, if he were known to have eaten, even when starving, a morsel of food which had been prepared by a Christian, the consequences would be dreadful. Where the Roman Catholic religion is in vigour, a man who should indulge himself in animal food on forbidden days would be regarded with horror. The use of wine, however moderate, would render a Mahomedan execrable to the whole of his tribe.

This misdirection of the favourable and unfavourable sentiments of mankind, in other words, this perversion and corruption of their moral sentiments, has, in by far the greater number of instances, been the work of priests, contriving the means of increasing their influence. In some very important instances, such, for example, as the prejudices of birth, at one time in Europe so powerful as to make men of low birth objects of the greatest contempt, men of elevated birth objects of the highest veneration, the perversion of the moral sentiments is evidently the work of the aristocratical class, securing to themselves a more easy dominion over the rest of their fellow-creatures.

It is, therefore, evident, that where antipathies, religious or aristocratical, should prevail, the press would be hurtfully employed in giving notoriety to the facts which would expose a man to the operation of either.

We have now ascertained the cases in which it would not be good that men should be protected from the declaration of truth by the press, and also the cases in which it *would* be good that they should be so protected.

What, upon this view of the subject, would be desirable, is sufficiently clear. It would be desirable that, in the one set of cases, the declaration should be allowed, in the other it should not be allowed. Are the two sets of cases, however, capable of being accurately distinguished?

If the comparison is made with any attention, it will not be difficult to determine that the evil to be incurred by the loss of truth in the set of cases in which the declaration of it would be useful, is much greater than that which would arise from permitting the declaration in the cases in which it would be hurtful.

In the first place, the set of cases in which the declaration would be useful are much more numerous, and much more important, than those in which, in any tolerably civilized state of society, it would be hurtful. Those in which it would be useful embrace the whole field of morality, all those acts, the performance of which, on account of their singular importance, has been elevated to the rank of virtues. Every body believes and proclaims, that the universal practice of the moral virtues would ensure the highest measure of human happiness; no one doubts that the misery which, to so deplorable a degree, overspreads the globe, while men injure men, and instead of helping and benefiting, supplant, defraud, mislead, pillage, and oppress, one another, would thus be nearly exterminated, and something better than the dreams of the golden age would be realized upon earth. Toward the attainment of this most desirable state of things, nothing in the world is capable of contributing so much as the full exercise of truth upon all immoral actions,—all actions, the practice of which is calculated to lessen the amount of human happiness. According to this view, the justice of which it is impossible to dispute, the evil incurred by forbidding the declaration of truth upon all immoral actions is incalculable. That which would be incurred by the antipathies of misguided minds against actions innocent in themselves, nobody, we should imagine, would so much as think of placing in comparison.

In our own country, for example, the classes of actions which, though they injure nobody, expose a man to the unfavourable sentiments of others, are not numerous. The number of persons who would be exposed to inconvenience on account of the declaration of truth, in regard to them, would be small in comparison with those who would benefit by its declaration, in the case of all really hurtful acts.

It is, indeed, important to be observed, that a comparative smallness of number is necessarily implied in the supposition of injury from any unfounded antipathy. Those who share in the antipathy, of course, abstain from the action. And unless the antipathy were so general as to include almost the whole of the society, it would lose its injurious effect. Besides, all the injury which can be done to the individuals against whom truth would in this manner operate injuriously, would be, to make them abstain from the acts which were thus condemned.

Another thing to be considered is, that the whole of the evil arising from the exercise of truth is dependent upon an accidental circumstance, capable of being removed; upon a mental disease, requiring to be cured, which, the legislature ought to be constantly endeavouring to cure, and toward the cure of which truth is likely to operate as the most effectual of all expedients. If any considerable inconvenience were experienced from exposure to unfounded antipathies, in consequence of the publication of truth, the groundlessness of these antipathies could not fail in this case to be so often canvassed, and made to appear, that at last it would become familiar to the multitude, and the antipathies would expire.

It clearly, therefore, appears, that, if the cases in 'which the declaration of truth would expose to unfounded prejudices could not be clearly defined, and separated from the cases in which the declaration would be salutary, the rule of permitting truth ought to be universal.' But though we perceive, that, to a considerable extent, there are cases, in respect to which it would be vain to hope for agreement in drawing the line of distinction between what is hurtful and what is not, we are persuaded that principles might be laid down in which all would agree, and which would serve to mark out certain cases for exception with sufficient exactness. If any such cases could be separated, either of actions which, though injurious to nobody, excited antipathies, or of facts, as those of birth, for which, though a man was in no respect worse, he might be regarded as worse; the exercise of truth, with regard to them, might, on the express ground that they were actions innoxious, or facts which ought to be of no importance in the estimate of human worth, be forbidden, when injurious, under the penalty of at least making reparation for all the injury of which it had been the cause.

III.

Offences of the Press with respect to Government.

We have now explained, we trust, with sufficient clearness for the present occasion, the principles upon which laws should be constructed for protecting the *rights of individuals* against violations committed by the press. The first part of this inquiry, therefore, we must consider as completed. In the second part we have to explain the principles upon which they should be constructed for protecting *the operations of government*.

Exhortations to obstruct the operations of Government in detail, should; Exhortations to resist all the powers of Government at once should not, be considered offences.

Unless a door is left open to resistance of the government, in the largest sense of the word, the doctrine of passive obedience is adopted; and the consequence is, the universal prevalence of misgovernment, ensuring the misery and degradation of the people. On the other hand, unless the operations of government, instituted for the protection of rights, are secured from obstruction, the security of rights, and all the advantages dependent upon the existence of government, are at an end. Between these two securities, both necessary to obtain the benefits of good government, there appears to be such a contrariety, that the one can only be obtained by the sacrifice of the other.

As this difficulty, however, arises chiefly from the largeness of the terms, a close inspection of the cases which they involve, and which they have a tendency to confuse, will enable us to discover the course which it belongs to practical wisdom to pursue.

It is necessary, first of all, to ascertain what sort of obstructions are inconsistent, and what are not inconsistent, with those operations of government, which are necessary for the protection of rights.

The application of physical force, to resist the government in applying to the execution of the laws the physical power placed at its disposal by the law, is such an obstruction of the operations of government, as would, if frequent, render it inadequate to the ends which it is provided to secure. This application of force, therefore, must be treated as an offence; and any thing proceeding from the press, tending directly to produce it, as a similar offence.

This proposition requires to be illustrated. The application of physical force which is here described, and treated as an evil, is clearly distinguishable from that resistance of government which is the last security of the many against the misconduct of the few. This is an application of physical force to obstruct the operations of government in detail; the proceedings, for example, of a court of justice; the proceedings of the legislative organ, or the proceedings of any of the administrative functionaries, in the execution of the duties with which they are charged. This is not that species of resistance which is necessary, in the last resort, to secure the people against the abuse of the powers of government. This last is not a resistance to the operations of government in detail. It is a resistance to all the powers of government at once, either to withdraw them from the hands in which they have hitherto been deposited, or greatly to modify the terms upon which they are held.

Even this last species of resistance it may be necessary to punish, at least in a certain degree, whenever it is not successful; that society may not be disturbed by commotions which the majority of the people disapprove. This, however, is a question which belongs to the penal code in general, and does not concern the inquiry into the offences capable of being committed by the press: because we think it may be satisfactorily shown, that no operation of the press, however directly exhorting to this species of resistance, ought to be treated as an offence.

The reason is, that no such exhortation can have any immediate, or formidable effect; can, indeed, have any effect at all, except through such mediums as ought to be at all times perfectly free. Suppose that a work is published, exhorting the people in general to take arms against the government, for the purpose of altering it against the consent of its rulers. The people cannot take arms against the government without the certainty of being immediately crushed, unless there has been already created a general consent. If this consent exists in such perfection as to want nothing to begin action but an exhortation, nothing can prevent the exhortation; and forbidding it is useless. If the consent does not exist in nearly the last degree of perfection, a mere exhortation, read in print, can have no effect which is worth regarding. In all circumstances, therefore, it is useless, and consequently absurd, to treat this species of exhortation as an offence. If, on the other hand, it were clearly recognized, that every man had a licence to exhort the people to the general resistance of the government, all such exhortations would become ridiculous, unless on those rare and extreme occasions, on which no prohibitions, and no penalties, can or ought to prevent them. The doctrine of this paragraph, which will appear somewhat startling and paradoxical to minds accustomed only to a certain train of ideas, will receive illustration, and we trust will be amply confirmed, as we proceed.

Having mentioned this as a grand exception, we now return to the cases in which not only physical force applied to obstruct the operations of government, but the publishing of exhortations to tha obstruction, ought to be treated as an offence. These relate solely, as above remarked, to the operations of government in detail. Obstructions, it is evident, may be offered to the operations in detail of a government which possesses and deserves the fullest confidence of the community at large; and the press may be employed in directly and efficiently exciting to these obstructions. A hand-bill, for example, distributed at a critical moment, and operating upon an inflamed state of mind, in a narrow district, may excite a mob to disturb the proceedings of a court of justice, to obstruct public officers in the execution of their duties, or even to disturb, on this or that occasion, the deliberations of the legislature itself.

These are clearly hurtful acts; they may be very accurately defined; and penalties, of moderate severity, would be sufficient to deter from the performance of them. Satisfaction by the party offending to the party injured, would often, in offences of this description, be out of the question; because there would be no definite party to whom an injury would be occasioned. It would only be necessary to ascertain the sorts of motives by which such offences would be liable to be produced, and to apply skilfully, as in other cases, motives of an opposite tendency, sufficient to counteract them. This would not be more difficult in this than in other cases, and it is not, therefore, necessary to explain at any length the mode of performing it.

One principle is to be carefully and most religiously observed, that of not imposing an atom of punishment for the purposes of *vengeance.* This is a principle, the justness and importance of which are so completely recognized, that we might have expected to be relieved ere now from the necessity of recommending attention to it. The fact, however, is, that so long as there are abuses in governments, so long will the men, who have the means of profiting by those abuses, exert themselves to multiply the list of offences against government, and to apply to them punishments of the greatest severity.

Punishments for contempt of court; punishments to vindicate the honour of the court, of the government, of the magistracy; punishments for the support of dignity; punishments severe in proportion as the dignity of the party offended is supposed to be high, and so on, are punishments almost always applied for purposes of vengeance, or the protection of the instruments of abuse. They are punishments, therefore, which will be rigidly excluded from a code which wisely and steadily pursues the general good.

Of Exhortations to obstruct the Operations of Government, in detail, there are two Sorts: 1. *The Direct,* 2. *The Implied, or Constructive.*

What the *sort of acts* are, to which the exhortations of the press ought not to be applied, has been so far ascertained. The next point is, to determine with accuracy what *sort of exhortation* it is that ought to be forbidden.

To all those who profit by the abuses of government, that is, more especially, to all those who, in a defective government, wield any of its powers, it is of great importance to leave as undefined as possible the sort of exhortation that ought to be forbidden. The point of greatest importance to them is, to keep the people at large from complaining, or from knowing or thinking that they have any ground of complaint. If this object is fully attained, they may then, without anxiety, and without trouble, riot in the pleasures of misrule: there is no limit to the degree in which the few may pursue their own advantage at the expence of the many.

There can be nothing, therefore, in which they have a greater interest, than preventing the press from being employed in any such way, as will lead the people to think that they have any thing, on the part of their rulers, of which to complain. All artifices possible will be sure to be employed to effect that prevention. And if it is enacted, that exhortations to acts which obstruct the operations of government in detail should be punished, *without defining accurately what sort of exhortations,* they will easily find expedients which, to a great extent, will accomplish their purpose.

Under the sort of constructions which it will be their interest to apply, every thing which can be done by the press, to make the people know or believe that there is any thing in the system of their government, or the conduct of their rulers, of which they have to complain, may be treated as an exhortation to obstruct the operations of government. Of these constructions, our experience affords innumerable examples. Does not the imputing of defects to the government, or misconduct to those who wield the powers of government, tend to bring both " into hatred and contempt?" And if the people hate and contemn the institutions and rulers of their country, will they not oppose their operations? The imputing of these faults, therefore, is it not, in essence and effect, an exhortation to oppose the operations of government? And are we to be governed, in our legislature, by the mere forms in which a set of words may appear, and not by our knowledge of their nature and consequences?

This is not only exceedingly plausible, but almost all the propositions which it involves are perfectly true. It is thus, therefore, the more easy to establish such a mode of interpreting an indefinite law of the press, as will prevent, or where the people cannot yet bear a total prevention, will go far towards preventing, whatever can lead the people to believe that any thing is amiss in the manner in which they are ruled.

There are two species of exhortations, one the explicit and direct, the other implied and constructive. In the one, a particular act is pointed out, and the party, or parties, addressed, are called upon to perform it. In the other, certain grounds are only laid, from which the opinion of the addresser, that the act ought to be performed, may, with more or less certainty, be inferred.

With respect to the first, there is no occasion for doubt. A direct and explicit exhortation to commit one of those acts, described above, as obstructing the operations of government in detail, should be treated as an offence. The precise question is, whether any exhortation, which is only implied and constructive, should be considered an offence? In the answer to this question, almost every thing which relates to the use of the press in matters of government, will be found to be involved.

Exhortations which are Implied and Constructive, ought not to be punished.

We have already divided the subject of resistance to government into two parts; first, that general resistance, the object of which is some great change in the government at large; and, secondly, resistance to this or that of its operations in detail.

We have already adduced an argument, which appears to us to be conclusive, to show, that no exhortation, whether explicit or implied, direct or indirect, the object or tendency of which is to produce the first species of resistance, ought to be subject to legal restraint.

It is necessary here to enter a little more fully into the grounds of that opinion.

We think it will appear, with sufficient evidence, that in the way of indirect exhortation to resistance, that is, in laying the grounds of dissatisfaction with the government, there is no medium between allowing every thing, and allowing nothing; that the end, in short, which is sought to be gained, by allowing any thing to be published in censure of the government, cannot be obtained, without leaving it perfectly free to publish every thing.

The end which is sought to be obtained, by allowing any thing to be said in censure of the government, is, to ensure the goodness of the government; the most important of all the objects, to the attainment of which, the wisdom of man can be applied. If the goodness of government could be ensured by any preferable means, it is evident that all censure of the government ought to be prohibited. All discontent with the government is only good, in so far as it is a means of removing *real cause* of discontent. If there is no cause, or if there is better means of removing the cause, the discontent is, of course, an evil, and that which produces it an evil.

So true it is, however, that the discontent of the people is the only means of removing the defects of vicious governments, that the freedom of the press, the main instrument of creating discontent, is, in all civilized countries, among all but the advocates of misgovernment, regarded as an indispensable security, and the greatest safeguard of the interests of mankind.

For what is meant by a vicious government? or wherein do the defects of government consist? Most assuredly they all consist in sacrificing the interests of the many to the interests of the few. The small number, in whose hands the powers of government are, in part directly, in part indirectly, placed, cannot fail, like other men, to have a greater regard for what is advantageous to themselves, than what is advantageous to other men. They pursue, therefore, their own advantage, in preference to that of the rest of the community. That is enough. Where there is nothing to check that propensity, all the evils of misgovernment, that is, in one word, the worst evils by which human nature is afflicted, are the inevitable consequence. (See the article GOVERNMENT.)

There can be no adequate check without the freedom of the press. The evidence of this is irresistible. In all countries, the people either have a power legally and peaceably of removing their governors, or they have not that power. If they have not that power, they can only obtain very considerable ameliorations of their governments by resistance, by applying physical force to their rulers, or, at least, by threats so likely to be followed by performance, as may frighten their rulers into compliance. But resistance, to have this effect, must be general. To be general, it must spring from a general conformity of opinion, and a general knowledge of that conformity. How is this effect to be produced, but by some means, fully enjoyed by the people, of communicating their sentiments to one another? Unless where the people can all meet in general assembly, there is no other means, known to the world, of attaining this object, to be compared with the freedom of the press.

It is, no doubt, true, that in countries where the liberty of the press is unknown, evil governments are frequently overthrown. This is almost always accomplished by the military force, revenging some grievance of their own, or falling in with some heat and animosity of the people. But does it ever enable them to make a new government, in which any greater security is provided for their interests than there was before? In such cases, the people get rid of one set of rulers, whom they hate, only to obtain another set, with equal powers of doing them injury.

There are, however, we believe, some people who say, that though the liberty of the press is a necessary instrument to attain good government, yet, if it is fairly attained, and if legal and peaceable means are in the hands of the people of removing their governors for misconduct;—if the people of England, for example, really chose the members of the House of Commons, and renewed their choice so frequently, as to have the power of removal after a short experience of misconduct, the freedom of the press would be unnecessary.

So far is this from being true, that it is doubtful whether a power in the people of choosing their own rulers, without the liberty of the press, would be an advantage.

Freedom of Censure on the Conduct of their Rulers, is necessary for the good of the People.

It is perfectly clear, that all chance of advantage to the people, from having the choice of their rulers, depends upon their making a good choice. If they make a bad choice—if they elect people either incapable, or disinclined, to use well the power entrusted to them, they incur the same evils to which they are doomed when they are deprived of the due control over those by whom their affairs are administered.

We may then ask, if there are any possible means by which the people can make a good choice, besides the *liberty of the press?* The very foundation of a good choice is knowledge. The fuller and more perfect the knowledge, the better the chance, where all sinister interest is absent, of a good choice. How can the people receive the most perfect knowledge relative to the characters of those who present themselves to their choice, but by information conveyed freely, and without reserve, from one to another?

There is another use of the freedom of the press, no less deserving the most profound attention, that of making known the conduct of the individuals who have been chosen. This latter service is of so much importance, that upon it the whole value of the former depends.

This is capable of being rigidly demonstrated. No benefit is obtained by making choice of a man who is well qualified to serve the people, and also well inclined to serve them, if you place him in a situation in which he will have preponderant motives to serve himself at their expence.

If any set of men are chosen to wield the powers of government, while the people have not the means of knowing in what manner they discharge their duties, they will have the means of serving themselves at the expence of the people; and all the miseries of evil government are the certain consequence.

Suppose the people to choose the members of the Legislative Assembly, with power of rechoosing, or dismissing them, at short intervals:

To what desirable end could these powers be exercised, without the liberty of the press? Suppose that any one of those whom they have chosen has misconducted himself, or promoted, as far as depended upon him, the ends of misgovernment; how are the people to know that the powers with which they had entrusted him had been treacherously employed?

If they do not know, they will rechoose him, and that as cordially as the man who has served them with the greatest fidelity. This they are under a deplorable necessity of doing, even to be just; for, as they know no difference between him and the best, it would be on their part iniquity to make any. The consequences would be fatal. If one man saw that he might promote misrule for his own advantage, so would another; so, of course, would they all. In these circumstances, we see laid the foundation on which, in every country, bad government is reared. On this foundation it is impossible that it should not be reared. When the causes are the same, who can expect that the effects will be different? It is unnecessary to dwell upon these fundamental truths, because they have already been developed in the article GOVERNMENT.

Without the knowledge, then, of what is done by their representatives, in the use of the powers entrusted to them, the people cannot profit by the power of choosing them, and the advantages of good government are unattainable. It will not surely cost many words to satisfy all classes of readers that, without the free and unrestrained use of the press, the requisite knowledge cannot be obtained.

That an accurate report of what is done by each of the representatives, a transcript of his speeches, and a statement of his propositions and votes, is necessary to be laid before the people, to enable them to judge of his conduct, nobody, we presume, will deny. This requires the use of the cheapest means of communication, and, we add, the free use of those means. Unless every man has the liberty of publishing the proceedings of the Legislative Assembly, the people can have no security that they are fairly published. If it is in the power of their rulers to permit one person, and forbid another, the people may be sure that a false report,—a report calculated to make them believe that they are well governed, when they are ill governed, will be often presented to them.

One thing more is necessary, and so necessary, that, if it is wanting, the other might as well be wanting also. The publication of the proceedings tells what is done. This, however, is useless, unless a correct judgment is passed upon what is done.

We have brought this inquiry, then, to an important point. In the article GOVERNMENT, we have seen that, unless the people hold in their own hands an effectual power of control on the acts of their government, the government will be inevitably vicious: We have now seen, that they cannot exercise this control to any beneficial purpose without the means of forming a correct judgment upon the conduct of their representatives: We have likewise seen, that one of the means necessary to enable them to judge correctly of the conduct of their representatives, is the liberty to every body of publishing reports of what they do. It remains to inquire, by what other acts the press can be made to contribute to the same desirable end.

What is wanted is, that all the people, or as many of them as possible, should estimate correctly the consequences of the acts proposed or done by their representatives, and also that they should know what acts might have been proposed, if the best were not proposed, from which better consequences would have followed. This end would be accomplished most effectually, if those who are sufficiently enlightened would point out to those who are in danger of mistakes, the true conclusions; and showing the weight of evidence to be in their favour, should obtain for them the universal assent.

How is this to be accomplished? In what manner are those wise men to be chosen? And who are to be the choosers? Directly the object cannot be attained. There are no distinct and indubitable marks by which wisdom, and less by which integrity, is to be known. And who is to be trusted with the privilege of pointing them out? They whose judgment requires to be directed are not well qualified to determine who shall direct them. And if the rulers are to choose, they will employ none but those who will act in conformity to their views, and enable them to benefit themselves by the pillage and oppression of the people.

As there is no possible organ of choice, no choice whatever ought to be made. If no choice is to be made, every man that pleases ought to be allowed. All this is indubitable. The consequences of denying any part of it are so obvious, that hardly any man, we suppose, will risk the imputations to which such a denial would justly expose him.

They who say that no choice ought to be made, say, in effect, that no limit whatsoever ought to be imposed upon the liberty of the press. The one of these propositions is involved in the other. To impose any restraint upon the liberty of the press, is undoubtedly to make a choice. If the restraint is imposed by the government, it is the government that chooses the directors of the public mind. If any government chooses the directors of the public mind, that government is despotic.

Suppose that, by the restraint imposed upon the liberty of the press, all censure of the government is forbidden, here is undoubtedly a choice. The government, in this case, virtually says, The people who might attempt the task of directing the public mind are of two sorts; one that of those who would censure; another that of those who would not censure; I choose the latter.

Suppose that not every censure, but only such and such kinds of censure, are forbidden; here, again, is still a choice, while confessedly there is no party to whom the power of choosing for the rest can with safety be given.

If not every censure, but only some censures, are to be forbidden, what are those to which the prohibition should extend? The answer to this question will elucidate nearly all that yet remains in any degree obscure, of the doctrine of the liberty of the press.

It will not be said that any censure which is just should be forbidden; because that would undoubtedly be to detract from the means of enabling the people to form correct judgments; and we have, we trust, rendered it indisputable that no source of benefit to society is at all to be compared with that of correct judgments, on their government and its functionaries, formed by the people, and determining their actions.

But what censures are just and what are unjust; in other words, what are the conclusions which ought to be formed respecting the properties and the acts of the government, is exactly the point to be determined. If you say that no man is to pass an unjust censure upon the government, who is to judge? It is surely unnecessary to repeat the proof of the proposition, that there is nobody who can safely be permitted to judge. The path of practical wisdom is as clear as day: All censures must be permitted, equally; just, and unjust.

Where various conclusions are formed among a number of men, upon a subject on which it would be unsafe, and therefore improper, to give any minor portion of them a power of determining for the rest, only one expedient remains. Fortunately, that is an expedient, the operation of which is powerful, and its effects beneficial in the highest degree. All the conclusions which have formed themselves in the minds of different individuals, should be openly adduced; and the power of comparison and choice should be granted to all. Where there is no motive to attach a man to error, it is natural to him to embrace the truth; especially if pains are taken to adapt the explanation to his capacity. Every man, possessed of reason, is accustomed to weigh evidence, and to be guided and determined by its preponderance. When various conclusions are, with their evidence, presented with equal care and with equal skill, there is a moral certainty, though some few may be misguided, that the greater number will judge aright, and that the greatest force of evidence, wherever it is, will produce the greatest impression.

As this is a proposition upon which every thing depends, it is happy that the evidence of it should be so very clear and striking. There is, indeed, hardly any law of human nature more generally recognized, wherever there is not a motive to deny its existence. " To the position of Tully, that if Virtue could be seen, she must be loved, may be added," says Dr. Johnson, " that if Truth could be heard, she must be obeyed." (*Rambler*, No. 87.)—" Je vous plains, mes Péres," says Mons. Pascal to the Jesuits, " d'avoir recours à de tels remèdes. Vous croyez avoir la force et l'impunité: mais je crois avoir la verité, et l'innocence. C'est une etrange et longue guerre que celle ou la violence essaie d'opprimer la verité. Tous les efforts de la violence ne peuvent affoiblir la verité, et ne servent qu'à la relever davantage: toutes les lumières de la verité ne peuvent rien pour arrêter la violence, et ne font que l'irriter encore plus. Quand la force combat la force, la plus puissante detruit la moindre: quand l'on expose les discours aux discours, ceux qui sont veritables et convainquants confondent et dissipent ceux qui n'ont que la vanité et le mensonge." (*Lett. Provinc.*

12.)—" Reason," says Burke, " clearly and manfully delivered, has in itself a mighty force; but reason, in the mouth of legal authority, is, I may fairly say, irresistible." *(Lett. on Regicide Peace.)*

It is of importance to show how many of the greatest men, of all ages and countries, have borne testimony to the prevalence of true over false conclusions, when both are fairly offered to the human mind. " Truth," says Mr. Locke, " certainly would do well enough, if she were once left to shift for herself. She seldom has received, and I fear never will receive, much assistance from the power of great men, to whom she is but rarely known, and more rarely welcome. She is not taught by laws, nor has she any need of force to procure her entrance into the minds of men." *(Letter on Toleration.)* The following is the emphatical language of Montesquieu: " La raison a un empire naturel; elle a même un empire tyrannique: on lui resiste, mais cette resistance est son triomphe, encore un peu de temps, et l'on sera forcé de revenir à elle." *(Esp. de Loix,* l. 28, ch. 38.)—" It is noted out of Cicero, by Machiavel, that the people, though they are not so prone to find out truth of themselves, as to follow custom, or run into error; yet if they be shown truth, they not only acknowledge and embrace it very suddenly, but are the most constant and faithful guardians and conservators of it." *(Harrington.)*—" The labour of a confutation," says Chillingworth, " I have not in any place found such labour or difficulty, but that it was undertakeable by a man of very mean abilities; and the reason is, because it is *Truth* I plead for; which is so strong an argument for itself, that it needs only light to discover it." *(Religion of Protestants.)*—" About things on which the public thinks long," says Dr. Johnson, " it commonly attains to think right." *(Life of Addison.)*—" The adversary," says Dr. Campbell, " is both subtile and powerful. With such an adversary, I should on very unequal terms enter the lists, had I not the advantage of being on the side of truth. And an eminent advantage this doubtless is. It requires but moderate abilities to speak in defence of a good cause. A good cause demands but a distinct exposition, and a fair hearing; and we may say, with great propriety, it will speak for itself. (Campbell *on Miracles,* Introd.)

We have then arrived at the following important conclusions,— that there is no safety to the people in allowing any body to choose opinions for them; that there are no marks by which it can be decided beforehand, what opinions are true and what are false; that there must, therefore, be equal freedom of declaring all opinions, both true and false; and that, when all opinions, true and false, are equally declared, the assent of the greater number, when their interests are not opposed to them, may always be expected to be given to the true. These principles, the foundation of which appears to be impregnable, suffice for the speedy determination of every practical question.

All censure thrown upon the government, all censure thrown either upon the institutions of the government, or upon the conduct of any of the functionaries of government, supreme or subordinate, has a tendency to produce resistance to the government.

Of the censures thrown upon government, some may have a tendency to produce resistance to the operations of government in detail; others that general resistance which has in view some great alteration in the government.

Of the first sort would be any such accusation of the conduct and disposition of a judge, as might excite the people, whose sympathies were roused in favour of the individual against whom his sentence was to operate, to rescue him from the officers of justice. We have already shown that such a rescue ought to be punished, and any direct exhortation to it ought to be punished. It will now be evident, we trust, that no censure on the judge, though capable of being treated as an indirect exhortation, ought to be punished.

The reason is conclusive. The people ought to know, if possible, the real qualities of the actions of those who are entrusted with any share in the management of their affairs. This they have no chance of knowing, without the unlimited power of censure upon those actions, both in gross and detail. To see the full force of these propositons, it is only necessary to apply the principles which have been already established.

If the people have not the means of knowing the actions of all public functionaries, they have no security for the good conduct even of their representatives. Suppose it is the duty of their representatives to watch the conduct of the judges, and secure the perfection of judicature, the people cannot know whether their representatives perform this duty, unless they know what the conduct of the judges is. Ignorance of this would of itself suffice to vitiate the government. A door would be left open, through which the rulers might benefit themselves at the expence of the people. All the profit to be made by an abuse of the power of justice, would thus become the profit of the representatives, by whom it would be allowed, and encouraged, as far as the knowledge, which they could not withhold from the people, would permit.

That the people ought, therefore, to know the conduct of their judges, and when we say judges we mean every other functionary, and the more perfectly the better, may be laid down as indubitable. They are deprived of all trust-worthy means of knowing, if any limit whatsoever is placed to the power of censure.

All censure consists in the delivery of an unfavourable opinion, with or without the grounds of it. This is the essence of censure. But if the conduct of the judge deserves that an unfavourable opinion should be entertained of it, the more perfectly that is known to the people, the better.

The conduct of the judge, on this occasion, says a defender, does not deserve an unfavourable opinion: A public expression of such an opinion ought, therefore, to be prohibited. But there are occasions on which the conduct of judges deserves an unfavourable opinion. When it is deserved, there is no security for good government, unless it is allowed to be made known. How can you allow an unfavourable opinion to be delivered in the one case, and not delivered in the other? To have the benefit of it in the one case, you must submit to the evil of it in the other.

In matters of Government, undeserved Praise as mischievous as undeserved Blame.

As the real point of importance is, to establish correct opinions in the minds of the people, it is as mischievous to inculcate a favourable opinion, when an unfavourable is deserved, as an unfavourable when a favourable is deserved; and, in the eye of reason, it is incontrovertible, that, if the one deserves to be prevented by punishment, so does the other.

But, if an unfavourable opinion is pronounced of any public functionary; of a judge, for example, would you have it left uncontradicted? Would you not grant the liberty of calling in question the truth of the allegations, and of supporting a different opinion? If not, the character of no public functionary would be safe, and any man, however deserving, might be made to appear the proper object of the most unfavourable sentiments. Why should not the two cases be treated equally? Why should not the favourable, as well as the unfavourable opinion be open to contradiction?

It is perfectly certain, that it is not in the power of law to mark out, by antecedent definition, any sort of men, of whom it can say, all opinions favourable to such men shall be punished. It can never be affirmed of any men beforehand that they will certainly perform such and such injurious actions. If they do perform them, all declarations conformable with the matter of fact are good. But the question is, whether they have performed them? One man, affirms that they have. Is that to be taken for granted? And is no man to be allowed to affirm the contrary, and to sift the grounds upon which the allegations of the other man are supported? It is by weighing well the evidence on both sides, that a well-founded opinion is capable of being formed. And it is certain, that the best security for having the evidence on both sides fully adduced, and the strength and weakness of it perfectly disclosed, is by permitting all those who are attached to different opinions to do what they can for the support of them.

If it is evident that it ought not to be permitted to speak evil of public functionaries without limit, while any limit is put to the power of speaking well of them; it is equally evident that, for the purpose of forming a correct opinion of their conduct, it ought not to be permitted to speak well of them, and oppose any limit whatsoever to the power of speaking ill of them.

It ought not to be permitted to speak evil of them without an equal liberty of speaking well; because, in that case, the evidence against them might be made to appear much stronger than it was. It ought not to be permitted to speak well of them without an equal liberty of speaking ill; because, in that case, the evidence in favour of them might be made to appear much greater than it really was. In either case, the people would be misguided, and defrauded of that moral knowledge of the conduct of their rulers, the paramount importance of which has so fully appeared.

It may be said (as by the short-sighted, if we did not anticipate them, it would be said), that if, by limiting the power of censure, the people are made to judge more favourably of their rulers than they deserve, the evil is small; but if they are permitted to form a very unfavourable opinion, the consequences are alarming.

We believe it may be rigidly demonstrated, that no evils are greater than those which result from a more favourable opinion of their rulers, on the part of the people, than their rulers deserve; because just as far as that undue favour extends, bad government is secured. By an opinion of their rulers more favourable than they deserve, is implied an ignorance on the part of the people of certain acts of their rulers by which the people suffer. All acts by which the rulers have any motive to make the people suffer, are acts by which the rulers profit. When the ignorance of the people extends to material points, all the evils of bad government are secured. These are the greatest of all possible evils. To this it will not be said that the ignorance of the people ought to extend. On all material points, it is admitted, then, that the freedom of censure ought to be complete. But if it is to be allowed on great points, on those where it is calculated to excite the greatest disapprobation; what can be thought of their consistency, who would restrain it on those where it is only calculated to excite a small? If it is proper to protect the people from great injuries at the hands of their rulers, by exciting a strong, it is good to protect them against small injuries, by exciting a weak disapprobation.

To public functionaries may be imputed either acts which they have not performed, or a want of certain qualifications, moral or intellectual, which they possess.

With respect to acts, and even dispositons, which do not, either directly or indirectly, concern their public function, the same protection may be safely extended to them as to private men.

Acts in their public capacity which they have not performed, may be imputed to them either by mere forgery, and without any appearance of ground, or they may be imputed with some appearance of ground. From permitting the former, no good can be derived. They ought, therefore, to be prevented, in the same way as false imputations, injurious to individuals in their private capacity. That there should be no restraint in imputing actions to any public functionary which he may appear to have done, flows immediately from the principles already established, and requires not that any thing should here be added to its proof. Any appearance sufficient to lay the foundation of the slightest suspicion, renders it useful to call the attention of the public to the suspected part, which can only be done by making the suspicion known. A man may, indeed, publish, as a matter of fact, what is supported by appearances which would only justify the slightest suspicion. In that case, he is sure of incurring the disgrace of temerity, if not of malignity; and this is all the penalty which needs or can safely be inflicted upon him.

In imputing inaptitude to a public functionary, on the score either of intellectual or moral qualities, scarcely any limitation would be safe. Every man ought to have liberty to declare upon this subject any opinion which he pleases, and support it by any evidence which he may think adapted to the end. If, in supporting his opinion of the inaptitude of any public functionary, he imputes to him actions which there is not even an appearance of his having performed, that limited prohibition, the propriety of which we have just recognized, will strictly apply. With this exception, freedom should be unimpaired.

We have now, therefore, explained, we hope sufficiently, in what manner the principles which we have established require, that the use of the press should be regulated in speaking of the action of public functionaries, and of their fitness for the duties which they are appointed to discharge, whether those functionaries are the immediate representatives of the people, or others whom it is the business of those representatives to control.

Freedom of Censure on the Institutions of Government is necessary for the good of the People.

We have next to inquire in what manner those principles require that the use of the press should be regulated in speaking of the *institutions* of government. The illustrations already adduced will supersede the use of many words upon this part of the subject.

Institutions of government are good in proportion as they save the people from evil, whether it be evil created by the government, or evil not prevented by the government. Institutions of government are bad in proportion as they are the cause of evil to the people, either by what they create, or what they fail in preventing.

According to this statement, which it is impossible to controvert, institutions of government may, in strict propriety of speech, be said to be the cause of all the evil which they do not save the people from, and from which the people would be saved by any other institutions.

It is therefore of the highest importance that the people should know what are the institutions which save from the greatest quantity of evil, and how much their own institutions want of being those best institutions.

Institutions of government are bad, either because those in whose hands the powers of government are placed do not know that they are bad, and though willing, cannot improve them; or they are bad, because those who have in their hands the powers of government do not wish that they should be improved.

Where the rulers are willing, but do not know how to improve the institutions of government; every thing which leads to a knowledge of their defects is desirable to both rulers and people. That which most certainly leads to such knowledge is, that every man who thinks he understands any thing of the subject, should produce his opinions, with the evidence on which they are supported, and that every man who disapproves of these opinions should state his objections. All the knowledge which all the individuals in the society possess upon the subject is thus brought, as it were, to a common stock or treasury; while every thing which has the appearance of being knowledge, but is only a counterfeit of knowledge, is assayed and rejected. Every subject has the best chance of becoming thoroughly understood, when, by the delivery of all opinions, it is presented in all points of view; when all the evidence upon both sides is brought forward, and all those who are most interested in showing the weakness of what is weak in it, and the strength of what is strong, are, by the freedom of the press, permitted, and by the warmth of discussion excited, to devote to it the keenest application of their faculties. False opinions will then be delivered. True; but when are we most secure against the influence of false opinions? Most assuredly when the grounds of these opinions are the most thoroughly searched. When are the grounds of opinions most thoroughly searched? When discussion upon the subject is the most general and the most intense; when the greatest number of qualified persons engage in the discussion, and are excited by all the warmth of competition, and all the interest of important consequences, to study the subject with the deepest attention. To give a body of rulers, or any other body of men, a power of choosing, for the rest, opinions upon government, without discussion, we have already seen, upon good evidence, is the way to secure the prevalence of the most destructive errors.

When institutions are bad, and the rulers would gladly change them if they knew they were bad, discussion, it will not be disputed, would be good for both parties, both rulers and ruled. There is, however, another case, and that by far the most common, where the rulers are attached to the bad institutions, and are disposed to do all in their power to prevent any alteration. This is the case with all institutions which leave it in the power of the men who are entrusted with the powers of government, to make use of them for their own advantage, to the detriment of the people; in other words, which enable them to do injury to the people, or prevent the people from good. This is the case with by far the greater number of those institutions by which the people suffer. They are institutions contrived for benefiting the few at the cost of the many.

With respect, therefore, to the greater number of defective institutions, it is the interest of the rulers that true opinions should not prevail. But with respect to these institutions, it is of still greater importance to the people that discussion should be free. Such institutions as the rulers would improve, if they knew that they were defective, will be improved as the rulers themselves become sensible of their defects. Such defective institutions as the rulers would not wish to see improved, will never be improved, unless the knowledge of these defects is diffused among the people, and excites among them a disapprobation which the rulers do not think it prudent to disregard.

That the prevalence of true opinions among the people, relative to those defects in their political institutions, by which the rulers profit at their expence, is of the utmost importance to the people, is therefore a proposition, which no improbity will dare openly to controvert. That freedom of discussion is the only security which the people can have for the prevalence of true opinions has already been proved. It is therefore proved, that freedom of discussion, in its utmost perfection, they ought to enjoy.

What is included in the term *freedom of discussion*, is evident from what has already been said.

Freedom of discussion means the power of presenting all opinions equally, relative to the subject of discussion; and of recommending them by any medium of persuasion which the author may think proper to employ. If any obstruction is given to the delivering of one sort of opinions, not given to the delivering of another; if any advantage is attached to the delivering of one sort of opinions, not attached to the delivery of another; so far equality of treatment is destroyed, and so far the freedom of discussion is infringed; so far truth is not left to the support of her own evidence; and so far, if the advantages are attached to the side of error, truth is deprived of her chance of prevailing.

To attach advantage to the delivering of one set of opinions, disadvantage to the delivering of another, is to make a choice. But we have already seen, that it is not safe for the people to let any body choose opinions for them. If it be said, that the people themselves might be the authors of this preference, what is this but to say, that the people can choose better before discussion than after; before they have obtained information than after it? No, if the people choose before discussion, before information, they cannot choose for themselves. They must follow blindly the impulse of certain individuals, who, therefore, choose for them. This is, therefore, a pretence, for the purpose of disguising the truth, and cheating the people of that choice, upon which all their security for good government depends.

If these deductions are as clear and incontrovertible as to us they appear to be, the inquiry respecting the principles which ought to regulate the use of the press is drawn pretty nearly to its close. We have shown, that as far as regards the violation of the rights of individuals, in respect to both persons and things, no definition on account of the press is required. We have shown in what manner the rights of individuals, in regard to reputation, should be defined by the civil code, and the violation of them prevented by the penal. We next proceeded to what may be considered as the main branch of the inquiry, namely, the use of the press in speaking of the institutions and functionaries of government. We have found, that in this respect the freedom of the press is of such importance, that there is no security for good government without it. We have also found, that the use of it, in respect to these subjects, admits but of two useful restrictions;—that of a direct exhortation to obstruct any of the operations of government in detail, and that of imputing to a functionary of government a criminal act, which there was no ground, nor even any appearance of ground, to impute to him. These restrictions, of course, it would be very easy to define in the criminal code, and to find appropriate motives to sanction. In all other respects, we have seen that the press ought to be free; that if there is any limit to the power of delivering unfavourable opinions, respecting either the functionaries, or the institutions of government, and of recommending those opinions by any media, with the single exception of false facts, under the circumstances mentioned above, the benefits which may be derived from the freedom of the press are so greatly infringed, that hardly any security for good government can remain.

IV.

Limitations to Freedom of Discussion, which involve its destruction.

In the administration of English law, or rather of what is called law, upon this subject, without being any thing better than the arbitrary will of the judges, it is said, that though discussion should be free, it should be " decent;" and that all " indecency" in discussion should be punished as a libel. It is not our object in this discourse to give an exposition of the manifold deformities of the English law of libel. If we have been successful in developing the true principles which ought to regulate the freedom of the press, every reader may, by an application of those principles, determine what he ought to think of the several particulars which there may attract his attention. We shall confine ourselves to a short notice of those *dicta*, or doctrines, which seem most likely to be pleaded in opposition to the principles which we have endeavoured to establish.

The question is, whether *indecent* discussion should be prohibited? To answer this question, we must, of course, inquire what is meant by indecent.

In English libel law, where this term holds so distinguished a place, is it not defined?

English legislators have not hitherto been good at defining; and English lawyers have always vehemently condemned, and grossly abused it. The word " indecent," therefore, has always been a term under which it was not difficult, on each occasion, for the judge to include whatever he did not like. " Decent," and " what the judge likes," have been pretty nearly synonymous.

Indecency of discussion cannot mean the delivery either of true or of false opinions, because discussion implies both. In all discussion there is supposed at least two parties, one who affirms, and one who denies. One of them must be in the wrong.

The delivery, though not of all true opinions, yet of some, may be said to be indecent. All opinions are either favourable or unfavourable. True opinions that are favourable to government and its functionaries will not be said to be indecent; nor will all opinions that are true and unfavourable be marked out for prohibition under that name. Opinions unfavourable may either be greatly unfavourable or slightly unfavourable. If any unfavourable opinions are exempted from the charge of indecency, it must be those which are slightly so. But observe what would be the consequence of prohibiting, as indecent, those which are greatly unfavourable. A true opinion, greatly unfavourable to a functionary, or institution of government, is an opinion that the functionary, or institution, is greatly hurtful to the people. You would permit the slight evil to be spoken of, and hence removed; you would not permit the great evil to be spoken of.

If no *true* opinion can be regarded as indecent, meaning by indecent, requiring *punishment*, we must inquire if any *false* opinion on matters of government ought to be treated as such. If all false opinions are indecent, all discussion is indecent. All false opinions, therefore, are not indecent. The English libel law does not treat any favourable opinions, how much soever false, as indecent. If all opinions that are false and unfavourable are said to be indecent, who is to judge if they are false? It has been already proved, that the people can confide the power of determining what opinions are true, what are false, to none but themselves. Nothing can resist the following argument. Either the people do know, or they do not know, that an opinion is false: if they do not know, they can permit nobody to judge for them, and must leave discussion its free course: if they do know, all infliction of evil for the delivery of an opinion which then can do no harm, would be purely mischievous and utterly absurd.

If all opinions, true and false, must be allowed to be delivered, so must all the media of proof. We need not examine minutely the truth of this inference, because it will probably be allowed. It will be said, however, that though all opinions may be delivered, and the grounds of them stated, it must be done in calm and gentle language. Vehement expressions, all words and phrases calculated to inflame, may justly be regarded as indecent, because they have a tendency rather to pervert than rectify the judgment.

To examine this proposition, it must be taken out of that state of vagueness in which so many things are left by the English law, and made, if possible, to speak a language, the meaning of which may be ascertained.

We have just decided, and as it appeared, on very substantial grounds, that the statement of no opinion, favourable or unfavourable, true or false, with its media of proof, ought to be forbidden. No language, necessary for that purpose, can be indecent, meaning here, as before, nothing by that term, as nothing can be meant, but simply *punishable*, or proper for punishment.

But the only difference between delivering an opinion one way and another way is, that in the one case it is simply delivered, in the other it is delivered with indications of passion. The meaning of the phrase in question then must be, that an opinion must not be delivered with indications of passion.

What! not even a favourable one?

" Oh, yes! a favourable one. Merited *praise* ought to be delivered with warmth."

Here, then, is inequality, and therefore mischief, at once. An opinion, meaning here a true opinion, if it is favourable, you allow—if unfavourable, you do not allow—to be delivered in a certain way. Why? Because in that way, you say, it is calculated to make an undue impression. Opinions favourable, then, you wish to make an undue impression, and by that confess the wickedness of your intention. You desire that the people should think better of the institutions and functionaries of their government than they deserve; in other words, you wish the government to be bad.

If opinions, to what degree soever unfavourable, may be freely and fully delivered, there are two conclusive reasons why the terms in which they are delivered should not be liable to punishment. In the first place, the difference between one mode of delivery and another is of little consequence. In the second place, you cannot forbid the delivery in one set of terms, without giving a power of preventing it in almost all.

First, the difference is of little consequence. If I say barely that such a functionary of government, or such an institution of government, is the cause of great injury and suffering to the people, all that I can do more by any language is, to give intimation, that the conduct of such functionary, or the existence of such institution, excites in me great contempt, or great anger, or great hatred, and ought to excite them in others. But if I put this in the way of a direct proposition, I may do so, because then it will be a naked statement with regard to a matter of fact, and cannot be forbidden, without overthrowing the whole of the doctrine which we have already established.

If, then, I give indication of certain sentiments of mine, and of my opinion of what ought to be the sentiments of others *explicitly*, I ought, you say, to be held innocent; if *implicitly*, guilty. Implicitly, or explicitly, that is the difference, and the whole of the difference. If I say, that such a judge, on such an occasion, took a bribe, and pronounced an unjust decision, which ruined a meritorious man and his family, this is a simple declaration of opinion, and ought not, according to the doctrine already established, to meet with the smallest obstruction. If I also state the matter of fact with regard to myself, that this action has excited in me great compassion for the injured family, and great anger and hatred against the author of their wrongs, this must be fully allowed. I must further be allowed to express freely my opinion, that this action ought to excite similar sentiments in other members of the community, and that the judge ought to receive an appropriate punishment. Much of all this, however, I may say in another manner. I may say it much more shortly by implication.—Here, I may cry, is an act for the indignation of mankind! Here is a villain, who, invested with the most sacred of trusts, has prostituted it to the vilest of purposes! Why is he not an object of public execration? Why are not the vials of wrath already poured forth upon his odious head?—All this means nothing, but that he has committed the act; that I hate him for it, and commiserate the sufferers; that I think he ought to be punished; and that other people ought to feel as I do. It cannot be pretended, that between these two modes of expression, the difference, in point of real and ultimate effect, can be considerable. For a momentary warmth, the passionate language may have considerable power. The permanent opinion formed of the character of the man, as well as the punishment, which, under a tolerable administration of law, he can sustain, must depend wholly upon the real state of the facts; any peculiarity in the language in which the facts may have been originally announced soon loses its effect. If that language has expressed no more indignation than what was really due, it has done nothing more than what the knowledge of the facts themselves would have done. If it has expressed more indignation than what was due, the knowledge of the facts operates immediately to extinguish it, and, what is more, to excite an unfavourable opinion of him who had thus displayed his intemperance. No evil then is produced; or none but what is very slight and momentary. If there should be a short-lived excess of unfavourable feeling, we have next to consider what is the proper remedy. Punishment should never be applied, where the end can be attained by more desirable means. To destroy any excess of unfavourable feeling, all that is necessary is, to show the precise state of the facts, and the real amount of the evil which they import. All excess of feeling arises from imputing to the facts a greater efficacy in the way of evil than belongs to them. Correct this opinion, and the remedy is complete.

Secondly, you cannot forbid the use of passionate language, without giving a power of obstructing the use of censorial language altogether. The reason exists in the very nature of language. You cannot speak of moral acts in language which does not imply approbation and disapprobation. All such language may be termed passionate language. How can you point out a line where passionate language begins, dispassionate ends? The effect of words upon the mind depends upon the associations which we have with them. But no two men have the same associations with the same words. A word which may excite strains of emotion in one breast, will excite none in another. A word may appear to one man a passionate word, which does not appear so to another. Suppose the legislature were to say, that all censure, conveyed in passionate language, shall be punished, hardly could the vices of either the functionaries or the institutions of government be spoken of in any language which the judges might not condemn as passionate language, and which they would not have an interest, in league with other functionaries, to prohibit by their condemnation. The evil, therefore, which must of necessity be incurred by a power to punish language to which the name of *passionate* could be applied, would be immense. The evil which is incurred by leaving it exempt from punishment is too insignificant to allow that almost any thing should be risked for preventing it.

Religion, in some of its shapes, has, in most countries, been placed on the footing of an institution of the state. Ought the freedom of the press to be as complete, in regard to this, as we have seen that it ought to be, in regard to all other institutions of the state? If any one says that it ought not, it is incumbent upon him to show wherein the principles, which are applicable to the other institutions, fail in their application to this.

We have seen, that, in regard to all other institutions, it is unsafe for the people to permit any but themselves to choose opinions for them. Nothing can be more certain, than that it is unsafe for them to permit any but themselves to choose for them in religion.

If they part with the power of choosing their own religious opinions, they part with every power. It is well known with what ease religious opinions can be made to embrace every thing upon which the unlimited power of rulers, and the utmost degradation of the people, depend. The doctrine of *passive obedience* and non-resistance was a *religious doctrine*. Permit any man, or any set of men, to say what shall, and what shall not, be religious opinions, you make them despotic immediately.

This is so obvious, that it requires neither illustration nor proof.

But if the people here, too, must choose opinions for themselves, discussion must have its course; the same propositions which we have proved to be true in regard to other institutions, are true in regard to this; and no opinion ought to be impeded more than another, by any thing but the adduction of evidence on the opposite side.

(F. F.)

THE ARTICLE

LAW OF NATIONS,

REPRINTED FROM

THE SUPPLEMENT

TO THE

ENCYCLOPÆDIA BRITANNICA.

LAW OF NATIONS.

I.

Ideas involved in the term Law.—These ideas how modified in the term Law of Nations.—The only sanction applicable to the Law of Nations is the popular sanction.—What dependence may be placed upon the popular sanction.

IN the meaning of the word Law, three principal ideas are involved; that of a Command, that of a Sanction, and that of the Authority from which the command proceeds.

Every law imports, that something is to be done; or to be left undone.

But a Command is impotent, unless there is the power of enforcing it. The power of enforcing a command is the power of inflicting penalties, if the command is not obeyed. And the applicability of the penalties constitutes the Sanction.

There is more difficulty in conveying an exact conception of the Authority which is necessary to give existence to a law. It is evident, that it is not every command, enforced by penalties, to which we should extend such a title. A law is not confined to a single act; it embraces a class of acts; it is not confined to the acts of one man; it embraces those of a community of men. And the authority from which it emanates must be an authority which that community are in the habit of obeying. An authority to which only a temporary obedience is paid, does not come up to the notion of that authority which is requisite to give existence to laws; for thus, the commands of a hostile army, committing plunder, would be laws.

The conditions, which we have thus described, may all be visibly traced, in the laws which governments lay down for the communities to which they belong. There we observe *the command;* there *the punishment* prescribed for its violation; and there *the commanding authority* to which obedience is habitually paid.

Of these conditions how many can be said to belong to any thing included under the term Law of Nations?

By that term is understood, something which either does, or which, it is supposed, ought to bind the conduct of one nation towards another.

But it is not understood, that one nation has a right to command another. When one nation can be commanded by another, it is dependent upon that other; and the laws of dependence are different from those which we are at present considering. An independent nation would resent, instead of obeying, a command delivered to it by another. Neither can it properly be said, that nations, taken aggregately, prescribe those laws to one another severally; for when did they ever combine in any such prescription? When did they ever combine to vindicate the violations of them? It is therefore clear, that the term Command cannot be applied, at least in the ordinary sense, to the laws of nations.

In the next place, it would not seem, that any thing, deserving the name of Sanction, belongs to them. Sanction, we have already seen, is punishment. Suppose nations to threaten one another with punishment, for the violation of any thing understood to be a law of nations. To punish implies superiority of strength. For the strong, therefore, the law of nations, may perhaps have a sanction, as against the weak. But what can it have as against the strong? Is it the strong, however, or is it the weak, by whom it is most liable to be violated? The answer is obvious and undeniable.—As against those from whom almost solely any violation of the laws of nations need be apprehended, there appears, therefore, to be no sanction at all.

If it be said, that several nations may combine to give it a sanction in favour of the weak, we might, for a practical answer, appeal to experience. Has it been done? Have nations, in reality, combined, so constantly and steadily, in favour of the law of nations, as to create, by the certainty of punishment, an overpowering motive, to unjust powers, to abstain from its violation? For, as the laws against murder would have no efficacy, if the punishment prescribed were not applied once in fifty, or a hundred, times, so the penalty against the violations of the law of nations can have no efficacy, if it is applied unsteadily and rarely.

On the mode in which it has been applied, we may appeal to a great authority. Montesquieu says—" Le droit public est plus connu en Europe qu'en Asie : cependant on peut dire que les passions des princes —la patience des peuples—la flatterie des ecrivains, en ont corrompu tous les principes. Ce droit, tel qu'il est aujourd'hui, est une science qui apprend aux princes jusqu'à quel point ils peuvent violer la justice, sans choquer leurs intérêts."—(Lett. Persanes, XCIV.)

To go a little deeper, we may consider, whether the interest of nations, that which, in the long run, governs them all, can ever produce combinations, from which an effectual sanction, of the nature in question, can be expected to proceed. That they would derive some advantage from the general observation of those maxims which have been called laws of nations, frivolous as are the points upon which the greater part of them turn, cannot be denied. These advantages, however, are seen at a distance, and with the mind's eye; they are speculative, rather than sensible.

The inconveniences, on the other hand, which must be felt, from any movement to lend effect to the law of nations, are immediate and formidable; the whole train of the evils of war are almost sure to arise from them. The latter class of impressions must, in general, be far more powerful than the former; and thus the interposition, in favour of the law of nations, will generally be shunned. A nation is often but too easily stimulated to make war in resentment of injuries done to itself. But it looks with too much coolness upon the injuries done to other nations, to incur the chance of any great inconvenience for the redress of them.

Besides, the object is to be gained by the means of combination. But the combinations of nations are very difficult things. Nations hardly ever combine without quarrelling.

Again, all nations ought to combine for an object common to all. But for all nations to combine in any one enterprise is impossible. Suppose a prince to have violated the law of nations, it would be absurd to suppose that all the countries on earth should conspire to punish him. But if not all, what is to be the selection? Who shall come forward; who stand excused? By those who are condemned to the sacrifice, in what proportion are the contributions to be made? Who is to afford the greatest, and who may come with the least?

It is unnecessary to pursue any farther the analysis of this extraordinary hypothesis. It is evident from what has been said, that it is full of impracticabilities.

Are we, then, obliged to consider the maxims or rules, which pass under the name of Laws of Nations, as utterly without force and influence; and the discourse which is made about them, as mere affectation and impertinence?

Not wholly so. It is of use, that the ordinary intercourse of nations should be conducted according to certain forms, generally known and approved; because they will be observed on all occasions, when there is no particular motive to violate them, and will often prevent disputes which might arise on frivolous occasions. They resemble, in this respect, the ceremonial of a court, or the established forms of polished society.

The objects, however, which are understood to be embraced by the law of nations, are of two sorts. The first are those minor objects, which partake more of form than of substance. The other are objects which deeply affect humanity. That there are certain interests of nations, which it were good to have considered as their rights, and of which it is infinitely to be desired that the violation could be prevented, is most true. But if national law has no penalty annexed to it; if the weaker party, who is wronged, has no means of redress; where, it may be said, is the advantage of such a law? Or where the propriety of calling that a law, which is only a declaration respecting rights; violated by the more powerful party with impunity, as often, and to as great an extent, as he pleases?

There is still, however, a power, which, though it be not the physical force, either of one state, or of a combination of states, applied to vindicate a violation of the law of nations, is not without a great sway in human affairs ; and which, as it is very nearly the whole of the power which can be applied to secure the observation of that law, deserves to be carefully considered, that, by duly appreciating its efficacy in this important affair, we may neither trust to it where it will disappoint our expectation, nor neglect the use of it where it may be turned to advantage.

That the human mind is powerfully acted upon by the approbation or disapprobation, by the praise or blame, the contempt and hatred, or the love and admiration, of the rest of mankind, is a matter of fact, which, however it may be accounted for, is beyond the limits of disputation. Over the whole field of morality, with the exception of that narrow part which is protected by penal laws, it is the only power which binds to good conduct, and renders man agreeable and useful to man. It is evident, also, that where there is not great inequality, it is a power, the binding force of which must be necessarily great. Because every individual, considered in himself, is weak and helpless as compared with the rest of the community. Unless, therefore, he can prevail upon them to abstain from injuring him, he must be exposed to unlimited suffering. And if, on the other hand, he can prevail upon them to combine in doing, or in desiring to do him good, he is put in the way of receiving perpetually the greatest advantages. His motive, therefore, to obtain the favourable, and to avoid the unfavourable regards of the members of the society in which he lives, is of the highest order. But he can obtain their favourable, and avoid their unfavourable sentiments, only by abstaining with scrupulous anxiety from doing any injury to them, and observing all such modes of conduct as are calculated to be useful and agreeable to them.

The value which men set upon these favourable regards of the persons among whom they live, is strikingly manifested by some of the most ordinary forms of their discourse and behaviour. What is more esteemed than character? What injury reckoned more deep and unpardonable than that of the man who exerts himself to take away unworthily any part of the reputation of his neighbours? But what is character, if not the title to the favourable sentiments of other men? And what is the loss of character, but the opinion of other men, that we do not deserve those favourable sentiments, with which they have been accustomed to regard us?

Honour and shame, those emotions, the intensity of which is proved by so many phenomena of human life, are but the feelings which attend upon those different situations. When a man finds himself in possession of the love, the esteem, and admiration of those by whom he is surrounded, he is filled with that delight which the belief of the secure possession of a great source of benefit, cannot fail to inspire: he is fearless, elated, and confident; the principal characteristics of that state of mind which we denominate pride. When he is conscious, on the other hand, of having forfeited in any degree the favourable sentiments of those among whom he lives, he suffers that depression which the loss of a highly valued possession is calculated to create; he ceases, in some degree, to look forward to his fellow men for good, and feels more or less the apprehension of evil at their hands; he fears to prove how far their disapprobation of him reaches, or to excite them to define it too accurately for themselves; he hangs down his head, and dares not so much as look them in the face.

When men are favourably situated for having those impressions deeply struck; or, more correctly speaking, when those combinations of ideas have consistently and habitually been presented to their minds, the association becomes at last so indissoluble and strong, as to operate, even where the connection among the things themselves may not exist.

When persons, who have been educated in a virtuous society, have, from their infancy, associated the idea of certain actions with the favourable sentiments, and with all the advantages which flow from the favourable sentiments of mankind; and, on the other hand, have associated the idea of certain other actions with the unfavourable sentiments, and all the disadvantages which flow from the unfavourable sentiments of mankind; so painful a feeling comes in time to be raised in them at the very thought of any such action, that they recoil from the perpetration of it, even in cases in which they may be perfectly secure against any unfavourable sentiments, which it might be calculated to inspire.

It will, we apprehend, upon the most accurate investigation, be found, that this is the only power to which we can look for any considerable sanction to the laws of nations;—for almost the only species of punishment to which the violation of them can ever become amenable: it is the only security, therefore, which mankind can ever enjoy for the benefit which laws, well contrived for this purpose, might be calculated to yield.

It is in the next place incumbent upon us to inquire, what dependence can be placed upon this security, in the set of cases now under consideration; and in what circumstances it is calculated to act with the greatest, in what with the least efficacy, toward this important end.

A power, which is wholly derived, from the good which may follow the favourable, the evil which may follow the unfavourable sentiments of mankind, will act most efficaciously upon him who is the most, least efficaciously upon him who is the least exposed to receive good and evil from the immediate inclination of his fellow men.

It seems to be evident, that he who is most weak, as compared with the rest of the community, is the most exposed to receive good or evil in consequence of their favourable or unfavourable sentiments; and that he, on the other hand, who is the most powerful, as compared with them, is the least exposed to receive good or evil in consequence of those sentiments.

When men are nearly upon equality, no one has any chance of inducing other people to abstain from hurting him, but by his abstaining from doing hurt in any way to them. He has no means of inducing them to do him any acts of service, but by their expectation of receiving similar acts of service from him. He is, therefore, intensely interested in its being generally believed of him, that he is a man who is careful to abstain from injuring, and ever ready to exert himself to do services to others.

The case is exceedingly different, where one man is lifted high above others. In that case he has powerful means of protection against their hurtful acts, powerful means of obtaining their services, altogether independent of his conduct, altogether independent of his disposition either to abstain from injuring them, or to render them service.

So far, therefore, as good conduct arises from a man's dependence upon the sentiments of others; and from this is derived the moral power, to which alone the term moral sanction or obligation can properly belong: the security for good conduct is apt to be lessened, in exact proportion as any one is raised above the level of those composing the mass of the community. If any man possesses absolute power over the rest of the community, he is set free from all dependence upon their sentiments. In this, or nearly in this situation is every despot, having a well established authority. So far as a man is educated as a despot, he can therefore have but few of those associations, on which a conduct, beneficent to others, depends. He is not accustomed to look—for the services which he needs, or the evils which he apprehends, from others—to the opinion which they may entertain of the goodness or badness of his conduct; he cannot, therefore, have that salutary train of transitions from the idea of an evil act to that of the condemnatory sentiments of mankind, and from the condemnatory sentiments of mankind to the forfeiture of all those delights and advantages which spring to him from the operation of their favourable regards;—associations which in men favourably situated become at last habitual, and govern the conduct, as it were, mechanically, without any distinct recurrence to the consequences, upon the thought of which, nevertheless, this salutary and ennobling sentiment ultimately depends, and from which it has been originally derived.

If such is the situation of the despot with regard to these important associations, it is in a proportional degree the situation of all those who partake of that species of elevation. In an Aristocratical country, for example, a country in which there is great inequality of wealth, those who possess the large fortunes, are raised to a great degree above any chance of receiving evil, or of standing deprived of any good, because the great mass, the lower orders, of their countrymen, think unfavourably of them. They are, no doubt, to a considerable degree dependent upon what the people of their own class may think of them; and it is accordingly found, that those qualities and acts, which are useful to that class, are formed into a particular, an Aristocratical code of morality, which is very effectually sanctioned by the favourable and unfavourable sentiments of the Aristocratical body, at the same time that it is exceedingly different from that more enlarged and all-comprehensive code, on which the happiness of the greatest number depends, and to which alone the epithet moral in propriety belongs.

Such being the state of the facts connected with this important case, it remains to see what are the inferences, bearing upon it, which we are entitled to draw from them. We have already ascertained, that the only power which can operate to sanction the laws of nations; in other words, to reward or punish any nation, according as it obeys, or as it disobeys them, is the approbation and disapprobation of mankind. It follows, that the restraining force is, in this case, determined by the associations which they who govern it may have formed with the approbation and disapprobation of mankind. If they have formed strong associations, of a pleasurable kind, with the approbation, strong associations, of the painful kind, with the disapprobation of mankind, the restraining force will be great; if they have not formed such associations, it will be feeble and insignificant. It has, however, appeared, immediately above, that the rulers of a country, of which the government is either monarchical, or aristocratical, can have these associations in but a very low degree; as those alone, who are placed on a level with the great body of other men, are placed in circumstances calculated to produce them. It is only then in countries, the rulers of which are drawn from the mass of the people, in other words, in democratical countries, that the sanction of the laws of nations can be expected to operate with any considerable effect.

II.

What is required to give to the Law of Nations its greatest perfection.—Necessity for a CODE *of International Law.—Rights of Nations.*

Having thus ascertained, what is the power which restrains from violating the laws of nations, and what the description of rulers upon whom its restraining force is the greatest, we are next to inquire, by what expedients the force of it may be raised to the greatest pitch, and the greatest amount of benefit may be derived from it.

It is sufficiently recognized, that whatever is intended to produce any effect as a punishment, produces it in a greater degree, in proportion as it operates with greater precision and certainty. The inquiry, then, regards the means of giving precision and certainty to those sentiments of the world, on which the binding power of the laws of nations so greatly depends.

Two things are necessary to give precision and certainty to the operation of laws within a community. The one is, a strict determination of what the law is, the second, a tribunal so constituted as to yield prompt and accurate execution to the law. It is evident, that these two are indispensible requisites. Without them no penalties can operate with either precision or certainty. And the case is evidently the same, whether we speak of the laws which regulate the actions of individual and individual within the state, or those which regulate the actions of one state towards another.

It is obvious to remark, in the first place, that with regard to the laws of nations, not one of these two indispensible requisites has ever yet had any existence. It has neither been determined what the laws in question are, nor has any common tribunal for cognizance of the violations of them ever been constituted. With respect to the last, not so much as the idea of it seems to have been entertained. And with respect to the first, though much has been written, it has been almost wholly in the way of vague and general discourse. Hardly a single accurate definition has yet been applied to any part of the subject.

Here, then, we come to what is obviously the grand inquiry; namely, *first*, What can be done towards defining the laws of nations? and, *secondly*, What can be done towards providing a tribunal for yielding prompt and accurate decisions in conformity with them? in other words, for applying with the greatest possible efficacy the opinion of the world for restraining the violation of them?

In the Article JURISPRUDENCE, to which it is necessary for us here to revert, we have sufficiently made it appear, that the foundation of all law is the constitution of rights. Of two parties, unless it is previously determined what each shall enjoy, it can never be determined whether one has improperly disturbed the enjoyment of the other. To determine, however, what a party is to enjoy, is to determine his rights.

Now, then, with regard to nations, the question is, what ought to be constituted rights? or in other words, what would it be desirable, for the good of mankind upon the whole, that the several nations should respect as the rights of each other?

This, it is pretty obvious, is one of the most extensive of all inquiries, far exceeding the limits of an article in the present work. We can attempt little more than to show the way in which the inquiry may be carried on.

In the Article JURISPRUDENCE, we have endeavoured to clear up the meaning which in legislation can, without leading to confusion, be alone attached to the term *Rights*; and we have there likewise seen, that there are but two classes of objects, in which individuals can have rights; namely, Things, and Persons.

The case, we believe, will be found the same with respect to nations. They also can have rights, in nothing but Persons, and Things. Of course, it follows, that they can receive injury in nothing but in Persons, or Things.

The inquiry, however, with respect to the rights of nations, is not so simple, as that with respect to the rights of individuals; because between individuals, subject to the same system of laws, the legislature recognizes no state of hostility; but between nations there is the State of War, and the State of Peace, and the rights which are understood to belong to nations are different in these two different states. In the state of war, nations recognize in one another very few rights respecting either persons or things; they kill the one, and take and destroy the other, with little other limit than the want of ability. In the state of peace, they respect as rights belonging to one another, nearly the same things which are constituted rights of individuals, by the ordinary systems of national law.

III.

What should be recognized as Rights in time of Peace.—The Property of Individuals.—The Persons of Individuals.—The Property or Dominion of the State.—Dominion in Land.—Dominion in Water.

We shall begin with the consideration of those things which it would be desirable that nations should respect as the rights of one another, in the time of peace.

And, *first*, of rights with respect to things. As the subject of the rights of nations, things may be divided into two sorts; things belonging to some individual member of the nation, and things belonging to the nation in its collective, or corporate, capacity.

Those rights in things which the nation guarantees to its individual members, within the nation, it would be desirable, with hardly any exception, that nations should respect in regard to one another; that those things, for example, which the government of the country to which a man belongs, would regard, and would compel all its subjects to regard, as his property, the governments of all other countries should respect, and compel all their subjects to respect as his property.

There are two states of circumstances in which questions may arise between nations, respecting the property of their respective subjects. The first, where the property in question, when the cause of dispute arises, is within the country of the individual to whom it belongs: The second, where the property has, by its owner, been previously removed into the country, with which, or some of the inhabitants of which, the dispute has arisen.

1. The first set of circumstances exists between two conterminous countries; the bordering inhabitants of which are neighbours to one another, and may, as any other neighbours, infringe the properties of one another. The proper mode of settling these disputes seems to be sufficiently obvious. The rights of the party complaining should be adjudged, according to the laws of the country to which he belongs. But the party sued or prosecuted, should be amenable only to the tribunals of the country to which he belongs; that is to say, the question should be tried before the tribunals of the country of the defendant; but the definition of the right in question should be taken from the law of the country to which the plaintiff belongs. It might in some cases be convenient for countries in this situation, to agree in constituting a common judicature, appropriated to these disputes, to consist, for example, of two judges, one of each country, with power to chuse a third, when they could not agree.

The injury complained of may be capable of redress by a remedy of the nature of a civil suit merely; or it may be of that more atrocious sort, theft or robbery, for which the remedy of punishment is required.

It would appear that punishment ought to be apportioned according to the laws of the country to which the party who has incurred it belongs.

Whatever would be the punishment decreed for the offence, if committed against a man of his own country, such a punishment he ought to sustain, for the offence against the man of the other country. The question of punishment is here understood, as extraneous to that of compensation. This ought always to be made to the party injured, where it is capable of being made, and in a case of property it is always capable; if not by the author of the injury, from want of property, or other cause, at least by the government of the country to which he belongs.

2. Where a man has removed his property from his own into another country, there seems to be no peculiar reason why it should be regulated by any other laws than those of the country into which he has removed it; why the rights which it confers should be otherwise determined; or the violation of them otherwise punished.

We have now considered, though in a very general manner (and our limits preclude us from attempting any thing more), the mode in which nations should agree about the rights of one another (in other words, the laws they should establish), in as far as the property of individuals, belonging to them, is concerned. After the *property* of individuals, their *persons* are to be considered as requiring the protection of laws.

There is more difficulty in determining what is desirable, as international law, upon this part of the subject, than in that which regards the property of individuals. It is desirable that the persons of the inhabitants of every country should receive protection, according to the laws of their own country. But it is also desirable that each man should sustain punishment according to the laws of his country; and these two objects are to a certain extent inconsistent with one another.

The inconvenience, however, seems to be greater, in permitting the inhabitants of one country to be punished, according to the laws of another; than in leaving the inhabitants of one country to the same measure of protection against injury to their persons from the inhabitants of other countries, as is afforded to the inhabitants of those countries by their own laws. Many cases, indeed, may be conceived, in which this is a measure of protection which all reasonable men would allow to be inadequate. In such cases, however, the only remedy seems to be the formation of a compact, by which a mode of proceeding, agreeable to the sentiments of both parties, may be positively prescribed. This latter expedient is of course extraneous to that equitable construction which ought to be uniformly applied by the tribunals of one country to the injuries perpetrated, by those whom they may have to judge, upon the inhabitants of another country. If an inhabitant of Persia, for example, should force cow-broth down the throat of an inhabitant and native of Hindostan, the tribunals of Persia should not punish this outrage, as they would punish one Persian for making another swallow the same liquid. To the Persian it would be a trifling injury, and more than a trifling punishment would not be required. To the Hindu, it would be one of the greatest of all conceivable injuries. It ought to be, therefore, put upon the same footing, with an injury of an equal degree, done to a Persian; the nature of the injury, not the external act, should be the object of consideration: and whatever the punishment which would be awarded against a Persian for one of the greatest injuries of which he could be guilty to a Persian, the same ought to be inflicted upon him, for this, one of the greatest which he could occasion to a Hindu.

Besides the cases in which a government, as representative of the country, may be injured through the individuals who live under its protection, there are cases in which it may be injured more directly. Certain things belong as property to the government, without belonging to any individual; and there are persons who are members of the government, or agents of the government, and who may receive injuries in that capacity, distinct from those which affect them, as private individuals. These are the cases to which it now remains that we direct our attention.

Those things which belong to government as goods and chattels; its moveables, for example; or the lands which it holds, as any individual holds them, in the way of an estate; there seems to be no reason for considering as subject to any other rules, than those applicable to the goods and chattels which belong to individuals.

Of other things, those to which any government can claim a right, as representative of a nation, must be, either, first, Portions of Land, or, secondly, Portions of Water.

1. The questions which relate to the rights which any nation may claim in any portion of land, are questions regarding boundaries; and these involve the whole of the questions respecting the acquisition of dominion.

To have any standard for determining questions with regard to dominion, the different modes of acquiring dominion, must be recognized; those which are proper to be allowed and respected by other nations must be distinguished from those which are improper, must be accurately defined and the definitions made known.

For this purpose it is easy to perceive, that the same process is necessary, as that for the definition of rights, described, at some length, in the Article in this work, entitled JURISPRUDENCE, to which we must again refer.

It is necessary, according to that example, that the events which are to be considered as giving commencement to a right of dominion, and those which are to be considered as putting an end to it, should be fully enumerated, and accurately defined.

This is the first part of the process. The other part is, to distinguish the different degrees of dominion. There is a dominion which is perfect, which includes every power over the subject in question, and leaves nothing farther to be acquired, a *dominium plenum*: there is also a dominion, which is but the commencement, as it were, of dominion, and includes the smallest possible fragment of a full dominion. These are the two extremes; and between them are various distinguishable degrees. All these should be fully depicted, and accurately defined.

When any of those events occurs which are to be considered as giving commencement to rights, it often happens that they are accompanied by circumstances which limit the right they would otherwise convey, and render the dominion less than full. These circumstances ought, also, to be completely enumerated; and the power of each to be accurately defined.

If this were done, an international code would be composed, in which the rights of dominion would be accurately defined; and to determine any question about boundaries, or about the degree of dominion, nothing farther would then be necessary than an adequate inquiry respecting the state of the facts.

The questions would exactly resemble those, which we have already described, in the Article JURISPRUDENCE, in analyzing what is called pleading in judicature. In a question about boundaries there is, let us suppose, a district, over which one country affirms that it has a right of dominion, a dominion more or less complete; and another country denies that it has that right. The first question is, Whether any of those events has occurred, which would give the affirming country a right of dominion? The second question is, Whether, if such an event had occurred, it was accompanied with any of those circumstances which limit dominion, and render it less than full, and if so, under what degree of limiting power they are classed? The third question is, Whether, if an event, thus giving commencement to a right of dominion had occurred, any other event, putting an end to that right, had subsequently occurred?

We need not here enlarge upon these several topics; because they will be sufficiently understood by those readers who bear in mind the expositions already given in the article referred to; and to those, who do not, we suggest the propriety of recurring to that article, as a preparation for the perusal of this.

It is evidently disproportionate to the limits which we must here prescribe to ourselves, to enumerate the events which it would be agreeable to the interests of mankind in general, that nations should regard as giving, and alone giving, commencement and termination to rights of dominion; because, in order to afford an enumeration which would be in any degree instructive, the reasons must be given why one set of events, and not another, should have the privilege in question conferred upon them.

It may be proper, however, in the mean time, to observe, that the events in question will not be found to be numerous, nor very difficult to discover. In fact, they are, and among civilized nations, almost always have been, pretty nearly agreed upon; and they are the questions of modification, and questions of fact, upon which, chiefly, differences have arisen. For example, there is no dispute, that Occupancy, where there is no prior right, is an event which should be considered as giving commencement to a right of dominion. Neither is there any doubt, that the Consent of those who have a right, may transfer that right to others: or in other words, that such consent is an event which gives commencement to a right in those others. Conquest, also, made in a lawful war, is recognized as an event of the same description; and, it will be found upon inquiry that these do, in fact, contain the whole. For on every occasion on which dominion is acquired, the territory so acquired must, before hand, either have belonged to some body, or have belonged to no body. If it belonged to nobody, occupancy is the only event which can be supposed to give commencement to the right. If it belonged to some body, it must be taken from him, either willingly, or by force. If it is taken from him willingly, we have his consent. If it is taken by force, it is by conquest in war, that the new right is created.

It is evidently, however, farther necessary, that the different species of consent should be distinguished; and those to which it would be proper to attach this investitive power, separated accurately from those from which it should be withheld. It is here accordingly, that the doctrine of contracts, would need to be introduced; that the different species of them applicable to this subject, in which all treaties would be included, should be enumerated; that the effects proper to be given to each of them should be defined; and the mode of interpreting them, or fixing the sense which they ought to bear, accurately laid down.

It would also be expedient, after the principal contracts, applicable to international concerns, are ascertained, to exhibit in the international code, *formulæ*, with blanks to be filled up, which should be employed by nations on all occasions of such contracts, and being framed with the greatest possible accuracy, would go as far as it would be possible by words to go, in excluding ambiguity, and the grounds of dispute.

With respect to conquest, the last event, calculated to give commencement to rights of dominion, mentioned in the above general enumeration, it is allowed, that as there are some conquests which ought not to be considered as conferring rights of dominion, there are others which ought to be considered as doing so. It is evidently necessary, therefore, that the line of separation should be drawn.

Whether a conquest, however, should or should not be considered as conferring a right of dominion, depends very much upon the nature of the war, through which it is made. If the war be what is regarded as just, and the mode of warfare conformable to the recognized rules, the conquest is apt to be regarded as conferring a legitimate title; if the war, and mode of war, be of a contrary description, the validity of the title conferred by the conquest may be liable to dispute.

It is evident, therefore, that in order to define the species of conquest on which the investitive power in question should be conferred, the circumstances which render a war justifiable, and the mode in which it is justifiable to carry it on, must first be ascertained. This forms the second part of our inquiry: and the question regarding the investitive power of conquest must be deferred, till that inquiry is performed.

2. Having thus far considered the mode in which should be determined the rights which nations acquire over portions of territory, or Land, it

remains that we consider the mode in which their rights should be determined with regard to Waters.

Waters, as concerns the present purpose, are, either rivers or the sea.

As the sea involves the questions of greatest extent and importance, we shall attend to that part of the subject first.

Even in the language of ordinary discourse, the sea is denominated the common domain of nations.

The first principle with regard to the sea is this, that all nations have an equal right to the use of it. The utility of recognizing this principle, is so apparent, that it has never been the subject of any dispute. And all the rights assigned to nations severally, in the enjoyment of this common domain, ought to rise out of this principle; and to be limited by it. Whatever use any nation makes of it, should be such as not to prevent a similar and equal use from being made by other nations. And every use which cannot be shown to have that effect, should be recognized as a right by the law of nations.

The principal use which nations make of the sea, is that of a passage for their ships. Agreeably to the principle which we have recognized, the ships of one nation should pass in such a manner as not to obstruct the passage of those of another. The rules according to which the possible cases of interference should be regulated, are very simple; and are, in fact, laid down and acted upon, with considerable accuracy. They resemble, in all respects, those according to which the vessels of the same country are made to avoid and to regulate their interferences in the rivers of the country, or upon its coasts. There would be no difficulty, therefore, in making accurate definitions of the requisite rights, for insertion in the international code.

The rights being established, the violations of them should be punished, on the same principles, as those which we have laid down in regard to the preceding cases. Either property has been injured, or persons. In either case, compensation is an indisputable part of the remedial process, wherever it is practicable. In loss of property it is fully practicable. It is also practicable in many of the injuries done to the person. As in the case of offences committed on land, the rights of the individual who has suffered should be estimated according to the laws of the country to which he belongs; but the punishment of the offender should be measured according to the laws of the country to which he belongs. In the case of piracy, which is robbery, or murder, committed by persons whom no country recognizes, and upon whom, therefore, justice can be demanded from no foreign government, it has hitherto been the practice that the nation suffering has taken the punishment into its own hands. Accordingly, the punishment of piracy has always been extremely severe. It would be, no doubt, better, if a mode were adopted, by which it would not be necessary for a nation to be judge in its own cause. A rule does not seem impossible to be framed, according to which the punishment of piracy might be provided for, by referring those accused of it, either to some general tribunal, constituted for that purpose, or to the tribunals of some nation other than that against which the offence has been perpetrated. A general law, on this subject, to be observed by all nations, would be highly desirable.

Rules, therefore, seem not difficult to be laid down, for regulating the proceedings of nations on the high seas. A distinction, however, is drawn between what is called the *high*, and what is called the *narrow seas*. By the narrow seas is commonly meant, some portion of sea, to a greater or less extent, immediately surrounding a particular country; and in which that country claims peculiar privileges. The question is, whether any such privileges should be allowed, and if allowed, to what extent?

The regulating principle in this, as in other cases, is the general advantage, the principle of utility. There are cases, in which certain privileges, in the waters surrounding a particular country, are of so much importance to that country; and the exercise of those advantages occasions so very little inconvenience to other nations, that what is lost, by all of them taken together, bears no comparison with what is gained by that particular nation. In these cases, the exercise of such privileges should be allowed; they should, however, be defined, in as many instances as possible, and promulgated by insertion in an international code.

Of the privileges in question, are all those which are essential, or to a considerable degree subservient, to the national security. In some cases, the exclusive right of fishing might perhaps come under the same rule. But this is in general provided for, by the necessity of drawing the nets, or curing the fish upon the land, a privilege which, of course, it is in the power of any nation to give or to withhold.

In obedience to this equitable principle, it appears, that such foppish privileges, as have sometimes been insisted upon, affording no advantage to one nation, which is not wholly at the cost of others—lowering the flag, for example, and such like impositions—should not be recognized by the code of nations.

It appears, also, that those tolls which have been, sometimes, and are levied, at the narrow inlets of some seas, deserve to fall under the same condemnation. The passage through these inlets is a common good to all the nations of the earth which may have a motive to use them; a good of the highest importance to the nations which are situated within, and to which it is the only means of maritime communication; and, while it imparts no evil to the coterminous nation, the toll which that nation levies is an advantage obtained wholly at the cost of others; and imposing upon them a burthen, in the way of obstruction and trouble, which is compensated for by advantage to nobody.

The waters, we have said, in respect to which rights should be assigned to nations, are rivers and the sea. Having stated what appears necessary on the present occasion with respect to the sea, it remains that we offer the few observations required, on the subject of rivers.

Rivers are either the boundary between two countries, or they are wholly within a particular country.

Those which are wholly within a particular country, it seems most agreeable to the principle of utility to regard as wholly belonging to that country In the case of navigable rivers which pass through several countries, it would indeed be desirable for those countries which are situated higher up than that at the mouth of each, as well as for all those who might thus have intercourse with them, that the navigation of such rivers should be free; but it would be difficult so to regulate this right, as not to affect the security of the country through which a free navigation should thus be allowed; and a slight diminution in its security would be so great a loss to that country as would require, to compensate for it, a very great advantage to those by whom the navigation was enjoyed. Unless where this advantage were very great, it would not, therefore, be agreeable to the principle which should dictate the laws of nations, that the freedom of the navigation should be regulated on any other principles than those of mutual agreement.

In regard to those rivers which flow between two countries, the principle of regulation is sufficiently plain. The benefits derivable from the river should be shared equally between them. Its principal benefits arise from the fishing and from the navigation. The right of fishing in most cases may be fitly distributed, by each party fishing from its own bank to the middle of the stream. The right of navigating of each must be so exercised as not to obstruct the right of the other. In this case the same sort of rules are required, to prevent the ships of the two nations from obstructing one another, in a common river, as are found available to prevent the ships of different individuals from obstructing one another, in a river belonging to one country. There is no difficulty, therefore, here, which it is worth stopping to show how to remove.

IV.

What should be recognized as Rights in time of War.—What should be regarded as necessary to render the Commencement of a War just.— What should be regarded as just and unjust in the Modes of carrying on a War.

We have now adduced, what our limits admit to be said, upon the first great branch of the inquiry relative to the law of nations; namely, the rights which they should recognize in one another in the state of peace. We proceed to the second branch, relating wholly to the state of war.

The questions which present themselves for solution relating to the state of war, are either those which respect its commencement, or those which respect the mode of carrying it on.

With respect to the commencement of a war, the principal question is, What are the conditions which should be regarded as necessary to render it just?

As men, in a situation where laws, and the protection derived from them, do not exist, are left to their own protection, and have no means of deterring other men from injuring them, but making them dread injury in return, so nations, which, with respect to one another, have, as we have seen before, but little protection from the legal sanction, are left to supply its place by this dread of injury in return, which, in the case both of individuals and of nations, may be called the *retributive sanction*, and of which, in the case of nations, war is the principal organ.

From this view of the essence and end of war, we lay down immediately one pretty extensive proposition with regard to the conditions necessary to render it just.

As the legal sanction, or punishment for the offences of individuals ought to operate only where some right has been violated, and the violation has been such as to require it, so the retributive sanction of nations, which is war, ought to operate only where some right of the nation, or something which ought to be treated as a right, has been violated, and where the violation has been such as to require that desperate remedy.

But as not all violations which may possibly be committed of the rights of a nation will justify it in inflicting war, the next object is, to draw the line of separation, and distinguish between those violations of the rights of nations which justify, and those which do not justify, the extremity of war.

As the evils which war produces are exceedingly great, it is, first of all, evident, that no violation of rights which is not very great, will, upon the principle which we have so often recognized, suffice to justify it. Of two evils, the least, is the choice of all sound legislation.

Of the violation of the rights of individuals, in the same country, the cases meet for punishment are capable of being pointed out, with a degree of accuracy, not wanting much of perfection. Of the violation of the rights of nations, committed by one nation against another, the cases which would justify the remedial operation of war are much more difficult to define. The difficulty, indeed, is not universal; for there are cases which may be very satisfactorily defined; and as far as definition can go, it is of the utmost importance that it should be carried. Uncertainty, then, pervades only one part of the field; which the more we are able to lessen, the greater is the advantage in favour of humanity. If a proper code of international law were formed, there would be certain defined violations of the rights of nations which would be pointed out, not only as deserving the indignation and hatred of all the world, but as justifying the injured nation before all the world, in inflicting upon its injurer the calamities of war. There would also be certain other injuries pointed out, of a more doubtful character, which might, or might not, according to circumstances not easy to define, be such as to justify recourse to war. The injuries of this secondary character, also, which might, or might not, according to circumstances, justify a war, are capable of being pointed out with a certain degree of accuracy. To a certain degree, likewise, the circumstances which would convert them into justifying causes, are capable of being foreseen. So far definition is capable of extending, and so far, of course, it ought to be carried.

In illustration of this latter class of injuries, we may select the most remarkable, perhaps, and important of all the instances; preparations for a threatened attack. A sense of security is one of the most valuable treasures of a nation; and to be deprived of that sense of security, is one of the greatest of injuries. But what state of preparation shall, or shall not be considered as justifying the threatened nation in striking the first blow, in order not to give its enemy the advantage of completing his preparations, and making his attack just at the moment when it would be most destructive, it is perhaps impossible to determine, for all cases, beforehand; though, no doubt, a certain progress may be made towards that determination, and the bounds of uncertainty may be greatly reduced.

We are aware how general, and therefore how unsatisfactory, these observations are, on the important subject of defining those violations of the rights of nations which ought to be regarded as justificatory causes of war; but at the same time it is to be observed, that not much more could have been done without framing the code, by actually enumerating and defining the violations for which that remedy should be reserved

Another consideration is now to be weighed. It is evident that whatever injuries are done by one nation to another, compensation may almost always be made for them. It is equally evident, that whatever injury may have been sustained, if compensation is made for it, the justificatory cause of war is removed.

The doctrine of compensation, therefore, is an important part of international jurisprudence. Before recourse is had to war, for any violation of rights, compensation ought first to be demanded; and no war, except in cases fit for exception, should be regarded as just, which this demand had not preceded; a demand which should be made through a constituted organ, and in a predetermined mode, as we shall more fully describe in a subsequent page, when we come to treat of an international tribunal.

As there can be no reason why the demand of compensation should not always precede the use of arms, except in cases of such a necessity as will not allow time for demanding compensation—a necessity for the immediate use of arms, in order to prevent an evil immediately impending—those cases of urgent necessity should, as far as possible, be sought out, and defined.

Other circumstances may be enumerated, as belonging to this first stage of the remedy, against a nation, which places itself in an attitude, affecting the sense of security of any of its neighbours. If a nation is making preparations, or executing any other measures, calculated to excite alarm, it may be called upon to desist from them; or it may be called upon to give security, that it will not make a hostile use of them. Of these securities, hostages are one of the most familiar instances. Various other instances will easily present themselves to the consideration of our readers. Upon this part of the subject, therefore, it is unnecessary for us to enlarge.

It thus appears, that we may lay down, with a considerable degree of precision, the conditions upon which the commencement of a war ought to be regarded as just. It remains, under this head of inquiry, that we show how it may, as far as possible, be determined, what ought to be regarded as just and unjust in the modes of carrying it on.

This is an inquiry of more complexity, a good deal, than the first. In looking out for a guiding principle, it is evidently necessary to keep in view the end to which every just war is of necessity restricted. That is, compensation for an injury received, and security that a fresh injury shall not be committed. Combining this with the grand principle of humanity and utility, in other words, of morality; namely, that all evil, wilfully occasioned, and not calculated to produce a more than equivalent good, is wicked, and to be opposed, we obtain one comprehensive and highly important rule; which is this: That in the modes of carrying on war, every thing should be condemned by the law of nations, which, without being more conducive, or more in any considerable degree, to the attainment of the just end of the war, is much more mischievous to the nation against whom it is done.

As the end is to be gained, in most cases, only by inflicting a loss of men and property, upon the opposing nation, it would be desirable that the distinction should be drawn between the modes of inflicting this loss, which are the most, and those which are the least calculated, to inflict pain and suffering, without being more conducive to the end.

One distinction is sufficiently remarkable; namely, the distinction between the men who are in arms or actually opposed to the designs of the belligerent, and the men who are not so; also between the property which belongs to the government of the opposing nation, and that which belongs to private individuals composing the nation.

With respect to the first class of objects, the men in arms, and the property of the government, there is not much difficulty. To produce the loss of them, as rapidly as possible, till the end or purpose of the war is obtained, appears to be a privilege which cannot be separated from the right of warring at all.

With respect to the loss of the men, indeed, there is an important restriction. It means the loss of them for the purposes of the war, and no more. If it be practicable to put them in a situation in which they can no longer be of any service to the war, all farther injury to them should be held unjustifiable. Under this rule falls the obligation, so generally recognized, of making our enemies, as often as possible, prisoners, instead of killing them, and of treating them with humanity, while retained in that condition.

That part of the subject, therefore, which relates to men in arms, and to such property as belongs immediately to the government, it is not impossible to include in rules of tolerable precision. The difficulty is, with respect to those individuals who, composing the body of the nation, form no part of the men in arms, and with respect to the property of such individuals.

Though it would not be correct to say, that these do not contribute, or rather that they may not be made to contribute, to the means with which the government carries on the war; yet it would be absurd not to recognize a very broad distinction between them, and the men and things which are immediately applied, or applicable to the war. A difference, therefore, equally broad, ought, in reason, to be made in the mode of treating them. The mode of treating the one ought to be very different from that of treating the other. As the rule of destruction must be the rule with regard to the first, only limited by certain restrictions; so the rule of forbearance and preservation ought to be the rule with regard to the latter, only to be infringed upon special and justifying circumstances.

Thus far we seem to have travelled with the advantage of light to our path. We may go a little farther, with equal certainty, and say, that as far as regards the persons of those who are not engaged in the immediate business of hostility, very few occasions can occur, in which it would be allowable, upon any just principle of international law, to do them any injury. Leaving them out of the question, we narrow it to the case of the property belonging to individuals; and shall now proceed to see how far the protection of it can be embraced within general rules.

We must suppose the case, which is the strongest, that of an invading army. The advantage which is capable of being derived to such an enemy, by seizing and destroying the property of individuals, bears, unless in certain very extraordinary instances, no sort of proportion, to the evil inflicted upon the individuals. This, we presume, cannot admit of a dispute. Upon the principle, therefore, so often recognized, as that, the dictates of which ought in this affair to be solely obeyed, no such destruction, unless in such instances, ought to be sanctioned by the law of nations. Such property, it is well known, can rarely be counted upon, as any considerable resource; because it is to a very great extent in the power of the people invaded to drive their property away, or to destroy it. The property of individuals, in an invaded country, would in general be a much more certain resource to an invading army, if that army were to purchase from them the articles which it desired. And, perhaps, this would be the most advantageous compromise, of which the circumstances admit; namely, that the invading army should abstain from the violation of private property; but that it should in return have the benefit of an unrestricted market; that nothing should be done on the part of the government of the invaded country to prevent its subjects from buying and selling with the invaders, as they would with any other parties.

It may no doubt be true, that the plunder and devastation of a province, or other portion of a country, must have an effect in diminishing the resources of the government for carrying on the war. In this point of view it must be allowed that the destruction of private property is of some importance to the invading nation with regard to the result of the war. But the question, in settling the difficulties of international jurisprudence, is not whether an advantage is gained, but whether the advantage, such as it is, be not gained, at too great a cost.

If it be certain that the losing party, in consequence of the destruction in question, loses more than the gaining party gains, it is certain that the two parties, taken together, are losers by the proceeding; and of course that nations, in the aggregate, are losers upon the whole. Nay, it is certain that each nation, taken by itself, is a loser, upon the balance of the cases in which it is liable to lose, and those in which it is liable to gain. If it loses more in the cases in which it bears, than it gains in the cases in which it inflicts invasion; and if it is as liable to bear, as to inflict, which is the usual condition of nations, it follows clearly that it is its interest to concur in a rule which shall protect the property of individuals, in cases of invasion.

Even in that more civilized mode, which has been adopted by invading armies, of availing themselves of the property of individuals; by exacting contributions through the instrumentality of the local authorities; contributions which these authorities are left to partition among the people, as they may deem equitable; though it is admitted that this is a much less hurtful proceeding than military rapine, still we think, it will easily appear, that the evil inflicted upon the contributors is greater than the benefits derived to the receivers.

Unless the amount thus received by an invading army is very considerable, the benefit which is derived, the aid which is gained towards accomplishing the end of the war, must be considered as trifling. But if a contribution, the amount of which can be of any considerable avail towards attaining the object of the war, is levied suddenly upon a particular district, a comparatively small portion of the invaded country, it must operate upon the contributors with a dreadful weight of oppression. Upon an equitable estimate of the circumstances, it can, therefore, hardly fail to appear, that, whether the contribution exacted is heavy or light (it must always be heavy to those who sustain it), the loss to those who suffer must greatly outweigh the advantage to those who receive. If it be so, this mode of exaction should, it is evident, be forbidden by the law of nations.

If these are the principles, upon which an international code, regarding this branch of the subject ought to be constructed, they will enable us to determine the question with regard to the property of individuals in another set of circumstances, to which the rules of civilized society have hardly yet begun to be applied. Whatever rules apply to the property of individuals found upon the land, the same rules ought, by parity of reason, it should seem, to apply to it when found upon the sea.

The conduct of nations, however, has hitherto not been conformable to the parity which appears to belong to the two sets of cases. Some tenderness, more or less, according to the progress in civilization, appears to have been shown, by all but savages, to the property of individuals upon the land. To this hour the property of individuals upon the sea is made prize of without mercy, by the most civilized nations in the world.

The notions of piracy, in fact, have, on this subject, unhappily prevailed, and governed the minds of men. Pirates make prey of every thing. Sailors, originally, were all pirates. The seafaring state was a belligerent state, of almost every vessel against every other vessel. Even when nations had gradually advanced into a more civilized state, and when their vessels abstained from injury to one another in a period of peace, they appear, when the ties of peace were dissolved, and they were placed with respect to one another in a state of war upon the seas, to have felt the force of none but their old associations, and to have looked upon the state of war as a state of piracy. Two nations at war with one another continue to act towards the property of individuals belonging to one another, exactly as two nations of pirates would do.

Assuredly this is a state of things, to which the present intelligence and morality of the world ought speedily to put an end. The very same reasoning which we have applied to the case of the property of individuals upon the land, is not less conclusive when applied to the property of individuals upon the sea. The loss to the party losing is more than an equivalent for the gain to the party that gains.

There is another consideration of great importance. All nations gain by the free operations of commerce. If then we were to suppose that the losses and gains of the two belligerent parties balanced one another, which yet they never do, there is an advantage derived from their commerce to every nation on the earth to which, in any degree, either directly or indirectly, that commerce extends; which advantage is either lost or diminished, by their preying upon the property of the individuals belonging to one another. This, therefore, is an unquestionable balance of loss, to the general community of nations, which the law of that community ought to endeavour to prevent.

If, then, we should suppose that it were enacted as the law of nations, that the property of individuals passing on the seas should be equally respected, in peace and in war, we may proceed to consider whether any disadvantage, nearly countervailing the general good, would thence accrue to the belligerents.

It may be alleged, that a nation at war with another is retarded in reducing its antagonist, by the riches which the commerce of that antagonist, if undisturbed, will place at its disposal. But it is evident that an advantage to one of two antagonists, when compensated to the other, by a power to overcome that advantage, exactly equivalent, is in reality no advantage at all. Such is the case with the advantage accruing to the nation with which another is at war, when the property of individuals upon the sea is allowed to pass unmolested. If its riches are increased by freedom of commerce, so are those of its antagonist. The advantages are equal, where the circumstances are equal, which, in the majority of cases, they undoubtedly are.

If it be still objected, that there may be cases in which they are not equal, the answer is obvious, and incontrovertible. There is no general rule without its exceptions, but partial evil must be admitted for general good. Besides, if the case were very remarkable, it might be excepted from the general rule.

If this were adopted as part of the law of nations, all those questions respecting the maritime traffic of *Neutrals*, questions which have been the source of so much troublesome inquiry, so much animosity, and so much mischief, would be immediately at an end. If the traffic of the belligerents, so far as concerned the property of individuals, were free, so would be that of all neutral nations.

Places actually blockaded, that is surrounded with an hostile force for the immediate purpose of being reduced, either by arms, or by famine, would still form exceptions; because the admission of ships into them, with supplies either of food, or munition of war, would be directly at variance with the very object of the blockade.

In all other cases, the admission either of provisions or of instruments of war into a belligerent country, ought, undoubtedly, upon the principle of utility, not to be disturbed. The benefit, except in rare and remarkable cases, could not be material to the country into which they might enter, nor hence the injury to its antagonist; on the other hand, that antagonist would enjoy the same privilege of the free admission of those commodities, and thus they would be equal in all respects. The inconvenience, however, which would thus be saved to the neutrals—the annoyance of search, the loss by detention, the occasions of quarrel—are known to be evils of no ordinary magnitude.

The desertion of sailors from the ships of a belligerent to those of a neutral has given rise to disputes in one instance only, that of Great Britain and the United States of America. The question to be determined, in laying down the principles of international jurisprudence, is, whether this desertion ought to be considered as constituting a ground for the general right of search; in other words, whether the evil to which a belligerent is exposed by desertion, or rather by that portion of desertion which can be prevented by the right of search, is an equivalent for all the evil which is unavoidably produced by it.

Desertion must take place either from the ships of war of the belligerent, or from its merchant ships.

In respect to ships of war, it is so easy for a belligerent to prevent desertion to neutrals, at least in any such degree as to constitute a great evil, that it would be altogether absurd to speak of it as fit to be compared with the evils arising from the right of search. The only occasions on which ships of war can be exposed to desertion to neutrals, must be those on which they go into a neutral port. But on those, comparatively rare, occasions, they can so easily take precaution against desertion, that the danger to which they are exposed is hardly worth regarding.

When the sailors belonging to merchant ships transfer their services to the ships of a neutral, it is not to be called desertion. It can only take place, in very considerable numbers, when seamen's wages in the neutral country are much higher than in the belligerent. The sailor, in this case, leaves his own for another country, only because he improves his situation by so doing. This is a liberty, which, as it ought to belong to every body, so it ought not to be withheld from the sailor. If, indeed, any nation thinks proper to forbid any class of its people to leave their country, as England with regard to its artificers, other countries cannot help that; but they ought not to be called upon to lend their aid to such an antisocial regulation, by allowing their vessels to be searched, as security against its infringement. Besides, it is evident, that there is a much greater security, arising from the very nature of the case, against the chance of a nation's being, to any considerable degree, deprived of its sailors by any such means. If the sailors go into the neutral country because wages are higher there, a small number only will have gone, when wages, from diminution of the numbers, will begin to rise in the country which they have left, and from increase of the numbers, will begin to fall in the country to which they have been tempted to repair. When the wages of seamen have thus sufficiently risen, in the belligerent country, which they are sure to do if the demand for them rises, the sailors will not only come back from every country in the world, but the sailors of other countries will hurry along with them; and the evil of desertion cures itself.

Only two questions, of any great importance, appear to remain; that relating to the march of troops, for a hostile purpose, through a neutral country, and that relating to the extent to which the operations of a successful war ought to be pursued.

According to the principles which we have already laid down for regulating the proceedings of a hostile army even in the invaded country, namely, that of committing no plunder, and enjoying the right of market, it appears that the right of passing through a neutral country on similar terms should be refused to no party. This rule, while it holds out equal advantages to all belligerents, admits, less than any other rule, grounds of dispute.

The end, which we have already described as that alone the pursuit of which can render any war justifiable, sufficiently defines the extent to which the operations of a successful war ought to proceed. The end of every justifiable war is to obtain compensation for an injury sustained, and security against the repetition of it. The last point, that of security, alone admits any uncertainty. Nations are apt to exaggerate the demand for security; to require too much; very often unconsciously, from the mere cravings of self-love; sometimes fraudulently, as a cover for ambitious views. As the question, however, respecting what may or may not, in each instance, be sufficient security, is a question of fact, not of law, it must be determined, if determined at all, by a tribunal empowered to take cognizance of the facts.

V.

Of the construction of an International Code, and an International Tribunal.—How the nations might concur in framing an International Code.—How an International Tribunal should be constructed.—Form of procedure before the International Tribunal.

We have now then laid down the principles by which, in our opinion, the rights of nations, in respect to one another, ought to be determined; and we have shown in what manner those principles should be applied, in order to come to a decision, in the most remarkable cases. The minor points it is, of course, not in our power to illustrate in detail; but that will not, we should hope, be difficult, after the exemplification exhibited, and the satisfactory solutions at which we seem to have arrived, of all the more considerable questions which the subject presents.

From what has been shown, it is not difficult to see, what would be the course pursued by nations, if they were really actuated by the desire of regulating their general intercourse, both in peace and war, on the principles most advantageous to them all.

Two grand practical measures are obviously not only of primary importance toward the attainment of this end, but are of indispensable necessity toward the attainment of it in any tolerable degree. These are, first, the construction of a Code; and, secondly, the establishment of a Tribunal.

It is perfectly evident, that nations will be much more likely to conform to the principles of intercourse which are best for all, if they have an accurate set of rules to go by, than if they have not. In the first place, there is less room for mistake; in the next, there is less room for plausible pretexts; and last of all, the approbation and disapprobation of the world is sure to act with tenfold concentration, where a precise rule is broken, familiar to all the civilized world, and venerated by it all.

How the nations of the civilized world might concur in the framing of such a code, it is not difficult to devise. They might appoint delegates to meet, for that purpose, in any central and convenient place; where, after discussion, and coming to as full an understanding as possible upon all the material points, they might elect some one person, the most capable that could be found, to put these their determinations into the proper words and form, in short, to make a draught of a code of international law, as effectually as possible providing for all the questions, which could arise, upon their interfering interests, between two nations. After this draught was proposed, it should be revised by the delegates, and approved by them, or altered till they deemed it worthy of their approbation. It should then be referred to the several governments, to receive its final sanction from their approbation; but, in the mean time, it should be published in all the principal languages, and circulated as extensively as possible, for the sake of two important advantages. The first would be, that, the intelligence of the whole world being brought to operate upon it, and suggestions obtained from every quarter, it might be made as perfect as possible. The second would be, that the eyes of all the world being fixed upon the decision of every nation with respect to the code, every nation might be deterred by shame from objecting to any important article in it.

As the sanction of general opinion is that upon which chiefly, as we have already seen, such a code must rely for its efficiency, not a little will depend upon the mode in which it is recognized and taught. The recognition should in each country have all possible publicity and solemnity. Every circumstance which can tend to diffuse the opinion throughout the earth, that the people of each country attach the highest importance to such a code, is to themselves a first-rate advantage; because it must be of the utmost importance to them, that all the nations of the earth should behave towards them upon the principles of mutual beneficence; and nothing which they can do can have so great a tendency to produce this desirable effect, as its being generally known that they venerate the rules which are established for its attainment.

If nations, then, were really actuated by the desire of regulating their mutual intercourse upon principles mutually beneficent, they would adopt measures for having a code of international law constructed, solemnly recognized, and universally diffused and made known.

But it is not enough that a code should exist; every thing should be done to secure a conduct conformable to it. Nothing is of so much importance for this purpose as a tribunal; before which every case of infringement should be tried, the facts of it fully and completely explored, the nature and degree of the infringement ascertained; and from which a knowledge of every thing material to the case should be as rapidly as possible diffused through the world; before which also all cases of doubt should regularly come for determination: and thus wars, between nations which meant justly, would always be avoided, and a stigma would be set upon those which justice could not content.

The analogy of the code, which is, or ought to be, framed by each state for regulating the intercourse of its own people within its own territory, throws all the illustration which is necessary upon the case of a tribunal for the international code. It is well known, that laws, however carefully and accurately constructed, would be of little avail in any country, if there was not some organ, by means of which it might be determined when individuals had acted in conformity with them, and when they had not; by which also, when any doubt existed respecting the conduct which in any particular case the law required, such doubt might be authoritatively removed, and one determinate line of action prescribed. Without this, it is sufficiently evident, that a small portion of the benefit capable of being derived from laws would actually be attained. It will presently be seen how much of the benefit capable of being derived from an international code must be lost, if it is left destitute of a similar organ. We shall first consider, in what manner an international tribunal might be constructed; and, next, in what manner it might be appointed to act.

As it is understood that questions relating to all nations should come before it, what is desirable is, that all nations should have equal security for good judicature from it, and should look with equal confidence to its decisions.

An obvious expedient for this purpose is, that all nations should contribute equally to its formation; that each, for example, should send to it a delegate, or judge. Its situation should be chosen for its accessibility, and for the means of publicity which it might afford; the last being, beyond comparison, the advantage of greatest importance. As all nations could not easily, or would not, send, it would suffice if the more civilized and leading nations of the world concurred in the design, with such a number of the less considerable as would be sure to follow their example, and would be desirous of deriving advantage from an instrument of protection, which to them would be of peculiar importance.

As it is found by specific experience, and is, indeed, a consequence of the ascertained laws of human nature, that a numerous assembly of men cannot form a good judicatory; and that the best chance for good judicial service is always obtained when only one man judges, under the vigilant eyes of interested and intelligent observers, having full freedom to deliver to the world their sentiments respecting his conduct; the whole of these advantages may be obtained, in this case, by a very effectual expedient. If precedent, also, be wanted, a thing which in certain minds holds the place of reason, it is amply furnished by the Roman law; according to which, a great number of judges having been chosen for the judicial business generally of the year, a selection was made out of that number, according to certain rules, for each particular case.

Every possible advantage, it appears, would be combined in the international tribunal, if the whole body of delegates, or judges, assembled from every country, should, as often as any case for decision came before them, hold a conference, and, after mature deliberation, choose some one individual of their body, upon whom the whole duty of judge should, in that case, devolve; it being the strict duty of the rest to be present during the whole of his proceedings, and each of them to record separately his opinion upon the case, after the decision of the acting judge had been pronounced.

It would be, no doubt, a good general rule, though one can easily foresee cases in which it would be expedient to admit exceptions, that the judge, who is in this manner chosen for each instance of the judicial service, should not be the delegate from any of the countries immediately involved in the dispute. The motive to this is sufficiently apparent.

We apprehend, that few words will be deemed necessary to show how many securities are thus provided for the excellence of the judicial service.

In the first place, it seems impossible to question, that the utmost fairness and impartiality are provided for, in the choice of the judge; because, of the two parties involved in the dispute, the one is represented by a delegate as much as the other, and the rest of the delegates are indifferent between them. In general, therefore, it is evident, that the sinister interest on the two sides being balanced, and there being a great preponderance of interest in favour of nothing but a just decision, that interest will prevail.

The best choice being made of a judge, it is evident that he would be so situated, as to act under the strongest securities for good conduct. Acting singly, he would bear the whole responsibility of the service required at his hands. He would act under the eyes of the rest of the assembled delegates, men versed in the same species of business, chosen on account of their capacity for the service, who could be deceived neither with respect to the diligence which he might exert, nor the fairness and honesty with which he might decide; while he would be watched by the delegates of the respective parties, having the power of interest stimulating them to attention; and would be sure that the merits or demerits of his conduct would be made fully known to the whole, or the greater part of the world.

The judicatory being thus constituted, the mode of proceeding before it may be easily sketched.

The cases may be divided into those brought before it by the parties concerned in the dispute; and those which it would be its duty to take up, when they were not brought before it by any of the parties.

A variety of cases would occur, in which two nations, having a ground of dispute, and being unable to agree, would unite in an application to the international tribunal for an adjustment of their differences. On such occasions, the course of the tribunal would be sufficiently clear. The parties would plead the grounds of their several claims: the judge would determine how far, according to the law, they were competent to support those claims; the parties would adduce their evidence for and against the facts, on which the determination of the claims was found to depend; the judge would receive that evidence, and finally decide. All this is so perfectly conformable to the course of pleading, and receiving proof, in the case of suits between individuals, as analyzed and explained in the Article JURISPRUDENCE, that it is unnecessary to be more particular here. If farther exposition is required, it will be found upon a reference to the article to which we allude. Decision, in this case, it is observable, fully accomplishes its end; because the parties come with an intention of obeying it.

Another, and a numerous class of cases, would probably be constituted, by those who would come before it, complaining of a violation of their rights by another nation, and calling for redress.

This set of cases is analogous to that, in private judicature, when one man prosecutes another for some punishable offence.

It should be incumbent upon the party thus applying to give notice of its intention to the party against which it is to complain, and of the day on which it means that its complaint should be presented.

If both parties are present, when the case comes forward for trial, they both plead, according to the mode described in the Article JURISPRU-

DENCE; evidence is taken upon the decisive facts; and if injury has been committed, the amount of compensation is decreed. When it happens that the defendant is not present, and refuses to plead, or to submit, in this instance, to the jurisdiction of the court, the inquiry should notwithstanding go on; the allegations of the party present should be heard, and the evidence which it adduces should be received. The non-appearance of the party defendant should be treated as an article of evidence to prove the truth of its opponent's allegations. And the fact of not appearing should, itself, be treated as an offence against the law of nations.

It happens, not unfrequently, when nations quarrel, that both parties are in the wrong; and on some of these occasions neither party might think proper to apply to an equitable tribunal. This fact, namely, that of their not applying to the international tribunal, should, itself, as stated before, be marked in the code as an international offence, and should be denounced as such by the international tribunal. But even when two offending parties do not ask for a decision from the international tribunal, it is not proper that other nations should be deprived of the benefit of such a decision. If these decisions constitute a security against injustice from one another to the general community of nations, that security must not be allowed to be impaired by the refractory conduct of those who dread an investigation of their conduct.

Certain forms, not difficult to devise, should be laid down, according to which, on the occurrence of such cases, the tribunal should proceed. First of all, it is evident, that the parties in question should receive intimation of the intention of the court to take cognisance of their disputes, on a certain day. If the parties, one or both, appeared, the case would fall under one of those which have been previously as above considered. If neither party appeared, the court would proceed to estimate the facts which were within its cognisance.

It would have before it one important article of evidence, furnished by the parties themselves, namely, the fact of their non-appearance. This ought to be considered as going far to prove injurious conduct on both sides. The evidence which the court would have before it, to many specific facts, would be liable to be scanty, from the neglect of the parties to adduce their pleas and evidence. The business of the court, in these circumstances, would be, to state correctly such evidence, direct or circumstantial, as it had before it; giving its full weight to the evidence contained in the fact of non-appearance; and to pronounce the decision, which the balance of the evidence, such as it was, might be found to support.

Even in this case, in which the practical effect of a decision of the international court may be supposed to be the least, where neither party is disposed to respect the jurisdiction, the benefit which would be derived would by no means be inconsiderable. A decision solemnly pronounced by such a tribunal, would always have a strong effect upon the imaginations of men. It would fix, and concentrate the disapprobation of mankind.

Such a tribunal would operate as a great school of political morality. By sifting the circumstances, in all the disputes of nations, by distinguishing accurately between the false colours and the true, by stripping off all disguises, by getting at the real facts, and exhibiting them in the true point of view, by presenting all this to the world, and fixing the attention of mankind upon it by all the celebrity of its elevated situation, it would teach men at large to distinguish. By habit of contemplating the approbation of such a court attached to just proceeding, its disapprobation to unjust; men would learn to apply correctly their own approbation and disapprobation; whence would flow the various important effects, which these sentiments justly excited, would naturally and unavoidably produce.

As, for the reasons adduced at the beginning of this article, the intention should never be entertained of supporting the decisions of the international court by force of arms, it remains to be considered what means of another kind could be had recourse to, in order to raise to as high a pitch as possible the motive of nations respectively to yield obedience to its decisions.

We have already spoken of the effect which would be produced, in pointing the sentiments of mankind, and giving strength to the moral sanction, by the existence of an accurate code, and the decisions themselves of a well-constituted tribunal.

To increase this effect to the utmost, publicity should be carried to the highest practicable perfection. The code, of course, ought to be universally promulgated and known. Not only that, but the best means should be in full operation for diffusing a knowledge of the proceedings of the tribunal; a knowledge of the cases investigated, the allegations made, the evidence adduced, the sentence pronounced, and the reasons upon which it is grounded.

The book of the law of nations, and selections from the book of the trials before the international tribunal, should form a subject of study in every school, and a knowledge of them a necessary part of every man's education. In this manner a moral sentiment would grow up, which would, in time, act as a powerful restraining force upon the injustice of nations, and give a wonderful efficacy to the international jurisdiction. No nation would like to be the object of the contempt and hatred of all other nations; to be spoken of by them on all occasions with disgust and indignation. On the other hand, there is no nation, which does not value highly the favourable sentiments of other nations; which is not elevated and delighted with the knowledge that its justice, generosity, and magnanimity, are the theme of general applause. When means are taken to make it certain that what affords a nation this high satisfaction will follow a just and beneficial course of conduct; that what it regards with so much aversion, will infallibly happen to it, if it fails in the propriety of its own behaviour, we may be sure that a strong security is gained for a good intercourse among nations.

Besides this, it does not seem impossible to find various inconveniences, to which, by way of penalties, those nations might be subjected, which refused to conform to the prescriptions of the international code.

Various privileges granted to other nations, in their intercourse with one another, might be withheld from that nation which thus demeaned itself in a way so contrary to the general interests. In so far as the withholding of these privileges might operate unfavourably upon individuals belonging to the refractory nations,—individuals who might be little, or not at all, accessary to the guilt, the effect would be the subject of proportional regret. Many, however, in the concerns of mankind, are the good things which can only be attained with a certain accompaniment of evil. The rule of wisdom, in such cases, is, to make sure that the good outweighs the evil, and to reduce the evil to its narrowest dimensions.

We may take an instance first from trivial matters. The ceremonial of other nations might be turned against the nation, which, in this common concern, set itself in opposition to the interests of others. The lowest place in company, the least respectful situation on all occasions of ceremony, might be assigned to the members of that nation, when travelling or residing in other countries. Many of those marks of disrespect, implying injury neither to person nor property, which are checked by penalties in respect to others, might be free from penalties in respect to them. From these instances, adduced merely to illustrate our meaning, it will be easy to see in what manner a number of considerable inconveniencies might, from this source, be made to bear upon nations refusing to conform to the beneficial provisions of the international code.

Besides the ceremonial of other nations, means to the same end might be derived from the law. A number of cases might be found in which certain benefits of the law, granted to other foreigners, might be refused to them. They might be denied the privilege of suing in the courts, for example, on account of any thing except some of the higher crimes, the more serious violations of person or property.

Among other things it is sufficiently evident, that this tribunal would be the proper organ for the trial of piracy. When preponderant inconvenience might attend the removing of the trial to the usual seat of the tribunal, it might delegate for that purpose the proper functionaries to the proper spot.

By the application of the principles, which we have thus expounded, an application which implies no peculiar difficulty, and requires nothing more than care in the detail, we are satisfied that all might be done, which is capable of being done, toward securing the benefits of international law.

(F. F.)

JC
223
.M64
1986
68534f